The Transsexual Scientist:

The Causation and Experience of Transsexualism and Transgenderism

Bevan Industries, Inc.

The Transsexual Scientist

Copyright © 2013, Bevan Industries, Inc.

Cover Art, Patricia Bell

danabevan@earthlink.net

The Transsexual Scientist:

The Causation and Experience of Transsexualism and Transgenderism

Dana J. Bevan, Ph.D.

This book is dedicated to my mysterious graduate school lecturer friend Julian Jaynes who taught me what it meant to be a psychologist.

Contents

PREFACE

I am a transsexual, but I am also a scientist by interest and training. I went through college and graduate school and learned that science funding for exploring the causes of transgenderism and transsexualism (TSTG) was unavailable in the United States. This was the era when Ellen Berschied won Senator Proxmire's mocking "Golden Fleece" award for a Federal grant to study why people fall in love. What constitutes politically correct basic and applied research on such issues has not changed to this date, but the rest of the world was not bound by our prudishness. Investigators from the Netherland, UK, Canada, Scandinavia and other countries pursued research on TSTG. Some US clinical psychologists and others did manage to bootleg some research in the US but "big" science, involving adequate financial resources for physiological studies, was not possible in the US.

It was only late in my career, after fighting the Cold War as a scientist and human factors engineer that I found out that there actually was a body of TSTG research work that I could analyze. I was given a teaching fellowship for one semester to teach college biopsychology while the regular professor was on sabbatical. There was less than 1 page on TSTG in the textbook but it was enough to get me started.

After 7 years of research and reading over 2500 research papers and after giving presentations at several scientific and TSTG meetings, I decided to write this book about the science and experience of TSTG. I decided to provide my TSTG history to help my colleagues, medical professionals and interested people understand the experience of being a TSTG and to organize the available scientific findings.

By nature and training I am inquisitive. So, be prepared for a personal and scientific detective story starting at age 4 as I gradually learned about TSTG and its causation. The autobiographical information is intended to give context to the science and the science is there because it is only through science that we can understand ourselves, whether TSTG or not.

To keep this book from being difficult to read, I have only provided citations for the most salient research reports. If you want citations on a particular topic, or more information please send me an email at danabevan@earthlink.net or go to my blog at http://biopsychologytstg. cniib.com/Biopsychology_TSTG/ or you can tweet me at @danajbevan or you can find me at http://www.facebook.com/dana.rees.5?ref=tn_tnmn

I want to thank my mentors L.G. and Julian Jaynes who taught me about science and the social institutions of science. I also want to thank my clinical psychologist for her support and understanding. I want to thank TSTG friends that gave me support, love and inspiration including M.P. and C.R.W. I want to thank Trisha for her art and understanding. Most important, I want to thank my true love.

CHAPTER ONE

Childhood and Child Rearing

*Your parents may have screwed you up in other ways but they did
not make you transgender or transsexual.*
-Anonymous

I was born in the post-WWII baby boom, not because by father was
away at war but because my parents had delayed getting my mother pregnant until things were more economically and socially stable. I was an
only child. There were two reasons for this. One, which was the public
reason given was that my mother was 33 when she had me, having gone
to college and taught school for several years. My uncle, who was also
our doctor, decided that at 33 years old it was too risky for her to have
any more children.

The actual reason for being an only child was that my father was afflicted with a chronic bone marrow infection and did not want to leave
my mother as a single parent. So he resisted having children. With today's
antibiotics my father could have easily been cured but he was afflicted as
a child, before modern antibiotics existed. The result was that one of his
legs was 5" shorter than the other, which in that day, without modern
prosthetic technology meant that he had to wear a "lift", sort of like a
stilt. It also meant that he hated doctors who had caused him so much
pain as a child. Although he walked with a limp, he was a vigorous man
who had always been passionate about sports and had been the manager
for his high school football and baseball teams.

During the depression, my father had to give up his dream of working on electronics when the RCA plant closed in the big nearby city.
Instead he and his family left their city house and moved to their country cottage to live off the land. There were few paying jobs. During the
war, my father farmed and did a lot of hunting, fishing and trapping,
in spite of his disability. This experience ultimately led him to work for

state government as a wildlife manager.

Because of his disability, my father was not drafted to fight in WWII, at least not in the military forces. Instead he supervised bombing and firing ranges that had been located in wildlife preserves. He helped create wooden mockups of ships and planes and military ground vehicle formations for practice with dummy bombs, unfortunately, mostly out of irreplaceable indigenous cedar trees. He also served as the local civil defense official and game warden.

Even after the war our family consisting of father, mother and only child, continued to live in the countryside. This was convenient for wildlife management, since the wildlife preserves started about a mile from our house. Our backyard became the command and logistics center for wildlife management in a large segment of the state, complete with vehicles, gas tanks and other equipment. Their most prized tools were some old surplus WWII heavy earthmoving equipment including a steam shovel, grader and tank retriever vehicle with a crane. All had ultra-powerful and noisy engines. I loved their power and their technical complexity.

Every morning my mother would get up early, long before leaving to teach school. She would make coffee and sometimes cook for the wildlife officers that met in our kitchen. My father gave the men their instructions and off they went for the day to convert former farmland and swamps into proper game preserves. They built hedgerows and planted appropriate vegetation for deer, rabbit, quail, pheasant and later even some wild turkey.

By all accounts and an occasional picture, I was a normal healthy, active boy. At the age of four, I was considerably taller and bigger than my peers and the size difference continued through elementary school. There weren't too many children to play with near our home, but my mother, being an elementary school teacher, taught me how to read and kept me busy with such "schoolwork" as I was capable of at my age. There was a steady flow of magazines into our house. Some of the magazines were our subscriptions and some were family hand-me-downs.

They were magazines like Life, American Weekly, Look, and National Geographic. I had my own bedside radio (courtesy of my father who had built it) and listened to it most every night including the news and entertainment programs.

Science and technology became magic to me. I could see it in the magazine articles on the atomic bomb, nuclear power, engines of war and civilian uses of technology. Later on Saturday mornings, I would watch US military propaganda on television such as the "Big Picture" that focused on high-tech engines of war. I discovered more science in magazine articles and became aware of its power to win a world war. I could see it in person in the powerful machines in the back yard that I spent hours exploring without permission.

Until I went to high school, I spent nearly all of my waking hours with my mother. During my early childhood, my mother stayed home to take care of me. She returned to teach elementary school when I went to kindergarten. She taught third grade in the same school I attended. It was all very convenient for commuting from our country house. It led to accusations of me being a "mommas boy" by my classmates and cousins. It meant that I was with her nearly all of the time, except for the Saturdays when my father would take me out in his pickup truck into the game preserves and woodlands to "check on things."

From all accounts, I was a curious child and asked a steady stream of questions of my parents. There was literally no one else to ask. Some were about science, while others were about the world away from our somewhat isolated country home.

Around age 3-4, I began to sense that something was terribly wrong with me. I had learned about the two gender categories from observing my family and others in my hometown, from looking at the pictures in the magazines and from the answers I got back from my parents. I knew a lot about gender and nothing about sex.

The answers I got to my questions about how males and females were supposed to dress and behave, confirmed my observations. Then I pressed my parents about personal concerns that undoubtedly caused my parents some anxiety. I told them, as best I could at that age that I did not feel like I was a boy.

My mother told me that I had no choice. I had a duty to play sports, grow up, get married and have a family. I would have to show courage in these activities. My mother would say that my father was an ideal man because he had done good manly things and showed lots of courage in dealing with his disability. I would be responsible for supporting a family and having grandchildren to carry on the family name. My mother would also be proud if I served in the military as my two maternal uncles had done during WWII. The responsibility of doing such things seemed a crushing burden to me but it also seemed far in the future. But at least I knew what I was supposed to do. For now, I only had to keep my secret from my parents because there were not many others around. In order to keep them happy, I learned masculine behaviors and pretended that I was a model boy.

I liked some things that boys liked: technology and powerful machines. But being a girl seemed more natural to me. I loved to read, sing, make pictures, and play records on my simple childhood record player. I played with the usual assortment of children's toys starting out with teddy bears but learned that dolls were forbidden because I was a boy, so I substituted ray guns and radios. I was especially fond of my record player with which I could play the Nutcracker and Swan Lake. I liked cooking and housekeeping with my mother, watching her sew and knit to create beautiful things and the clothing that hung in her closet. My mother would talk to me about skills in which I showed an interest, like cleaning and baking and sewing on a button, although I was not quite ready yet to practice these motor skills on my own until later. Sports were okay but there was usually no one around to play with. I would go out with a baseball bat and ball. I would hold the bat in one hand and throw up the ball with the other. After I hit the ball, I would run to where it had gone. I did not realize that I accomplished these things left-handed. It just seemed natural and there was no one around to tell me it might be wrong.

I had a wonderful, strong soprano singing voice, probably from my Welsh heritage. I was in demand to sing in church, at Christmas cantatas and school choruses. I was always the boy soprano singing "O Holy Night." When our junior choir sang together with the senior choir I did my best to shown the senior choir members that I had the better soprano voice.

When I did not understand the words in the magazines, I would look at the pictures in LIFE and LOOK, particularly those of fashionable ladies. But, it was not long before I could read most of the words due to my mother's tutelage. Long before kindergarten, I was a functional reader although I occasionally got "stuck" on words that I had not encountered before. I loved to play pretend with my neighbors, taking the part of the mother or the sister and sometimes the father. I loved the smooth fabrics that my mother wore and hated to wear my scratchy open-weave wool pants to church. On Sundays, I loved to wear bowties with long tails, like they used to wear in the old West, particularly in red. They made me feel special.

By this time, I had long since started secretly dressing in my mother's clothing, at least the items that I could reach. There was a cedar chest in her room with a drawer that was no more than a foot off the ground where she kept her girdles and shower cap and some panties. (This cedar chest now resides in my living room.) This provided easy access to me and as I grew taller I also managed to access her dresses and slips that were hanging in the closet. Her cosmetics were harder to access but she would frequently leave some of them in the bathroom on the toilet back. After I locked the bathroom door, I experimented with powder and lipstick while looking in the mirror. I learned to remove the makeup with cold cream to cover my tracks.

As I got even taller, I could access the bathroom cabinets and found additional cosmetics as well as a funny round rubber thing that I learned much later prevented me from having brothers and sisters. I experiment a few times with non-conforming clothing. Once I wore boxer underwear shorts to choir practice. I figured nothing was wrong with wearing them outside if I had two pairs turned around inside as underwear. I got as far as the church parking lot before my mother took me back home. I also learned from occasionally getting caught that there was something shameful and inappropriate for a boy to wear ladies clothes or use makeup.

The questions to my parents intensified as the story of Christine Jorgenson started getting radio time and magazine coverage in 1952. From their awkwardness in answering my questions, I sensed from my parents that there was danger here. I wanted to know why I could not grow up and become a lady. And I wanted to know why I could not wear ladies clothes, which I had already surreptitiously been wearing. Were there other boys and men who wore ladies clothing? Could I be a lady when I grew up like her (Christine)?

My parents responded that people who dressed in opposite sex clothing were not like us. Many of them were crazy and were put in the local state mental hospital. I already had first hand knowledge of people going off to the mental hospital. The teenage girl who used to live next door and occasionally had been my babysitter had been shipped off because she was crazy, not to be seen again. I learned that the mental hospital was like a prison with deranged people shrieking all the time and in that era that probably was accurate. It was not a pretty picture and that is probably what my parents wanted me to think.

I pointed out that Christine Jorgenson did not seem crazy but seemed elegant and nice and they started to backpedal. I finally backed them into a position that being like Christine was too serious for a child, like me to understand. When I was older, I could decide better what to do.

My mother and father answered all of these questions in a straight-forward manner. Although I detected occasional embarrassment, they never rejected my interrogatories or punished me for asking. I was their first child and they probably thought that these were normal questions for a child of my age. The questions about Christine were also embedded in the already numerous questions that I asked about a multitude of other things. From their non-verbal reactions I confirmed that the questions I asked about transsexuals were somehow dangerous and the subject was taboo. I had already been punished when I was caught dressing or wearing makeup but I had been punished for a lot of misbehaviors unrelated to crossdressing. It was different.

I was literally deep in the closet by age 5. From my parents answers I concluded that there was something wrong with me because I wanted to be a girl. I started to keep it a secret--a secret from my parents, my classmates, my cousins, my teachers and everyone else. I was trying to comply with my duties as a male and this was reinforced by the fear of being sent to a mental hospital.

About this time I first saw Milton Berle in drag on television. I was embarrassed to watch him in front of my parents. People were laughing at his attempts to caricature being a woman and I did not want to be laughed at in that way. His women presentations were hideous but my presentations were not much better. I saw myself being mocked if I actually dressed like a woman in public. Crossdressing was something to be laughed at because it was abnormal.

My secret life began. I had learned to withhold what I wanted to say and had started a life of secrecy that has not yet totally ended, some 60 years later. If my parents really suspected my discomfort with becoming a man they never said so directly. However, they had information from the time before I had started my secret life and I thought that they might suspect.

On the gender behavior front, things got worse when I hit kindergarten. Up until that time I had been sheltered by physical isolation from having to face the gender divide. The kindergarten regimentation of what boys were expected to do and not do and how boys and girls were kept separate and were played off against one another was a shock. Boys lined up here, girls over there. The best line would go to recess first. Boys played with the barrel "airplane", the blocks and the trucks. Girls played in the "house" area with a pretend kitchen and ironing board. As a boy, I was not to play with the girl things under penalty of shaming by the teacher and classmates. And my mother was teaching in a room upstairs, she would surely find out if I violated the rules.

By the end of the first week of Kindergarten, I had had enough. I bolted from the Kindergarten class during recess break. I went to my mother crying, but was upset that I was unable to tell her why. I had created a dustup of major proportions for the two teachers and the principal. By going AWOL I had violated the Kindergarten teachers responsibility to keep track of her class. By going to my mother, I had set a bad example for the pupils in the school, and the principal knew that I had three classmates whose mothers were also teachers in the school.

I was called before the principal in private. She was particularly scary because she was older than the teachers and talked with an edge. Even she was affected by a crying 5 year old on the first week of school. It was just the usual homesickness of going to school for the first time, or so she thought. At first I would not tell her why I was crying but then she started to get me to respond to a series of questions aimed at getting to admit that I had done something wrong. Was my behavior fair or unfair to my teacher and my mother? "Unfair." Was I being kind or unkind to them? "Unkind." Was it right on wrong to do what I had done? "Wrong." At first I gave into her arguments but then I started to fight back, continuing to cry. It was not right that I could not play with the girls and could not play with "their toys." It was not right to separate us into boys and girls groups.

Out of surprise, the principal suddenly stopped her interrogation. She was more used to 11-year old tough boys who had been caught smoking or fighting. She was not expecting a crying and now, angry 5-year old in her office essentially espousing mingling of the sexes and relaxation of gender stereotypes. I was so angry that I did not care who she was and I was only later fully aware of her authority. She seemed to understand why I was upset but did not say she was giving in to me. I was dismissed back to my class.

The principal resolved the situation by having my mother tell me that while she was teaching, she could not act as my mother. I was to stay in class with my teacher. I did not like that but the potential penalty was that my mother would have to give up teaching and I would have to go to an inferior school. Those penalties frightened me into acceptance. The kindergarten teacher announce that everyone could play with any of the toys or people during playtime and she never made a boy-girl separation again, changing to table groupings instead, since we did not sit at desks but tables with 8 places. At bathroom time, the girls would just peel off from their lines composed of tables 1, 2 and 3 or 4, 5, and 6 and go to their designated room and likewise for the boys.

For me, this is the first time that I had run up against the cultural forces trying to make me into a boy and isolating me from girls. It was also the first time that I had done anything publicly wrong, it made me scared and I did not like the experience. I had tried to stand up for myself but it took getting angry to do it. Although I eventually adapted to school sexual regimentation, the experience drove me further underground in regard to expressing my discomfort with being a boy.

In elementary and junior high, things got a little better on the sexual divide front. Both schools, to some extent, used homogenous grouping. Homogenous grouping allowed me to be with the girls because they were usually the good students like me. In elementary school, they had homogenous reading groups and I was always in the "red birds". The other two groups were usually the "blue jays" and the "orioles" although the teachers did their best not to reveal that these were the reading groups that needed more attention. Each group learned reading in a circle and they went on to do other activities as a group in a rotation. I had some wonderful girlfriends at school but was unable to play with them outside of school time because I had to return to my home in the country. Arranging boy-girl play dates was out of the question because "boys do not play with girls." In junior high school, I was too young for dating, although I did try to befriend girls.

Although we lived out in the boondocks, for a time I did have a girl playmate that lived close enough that I could walk to her house. We had a good time play acting, playing softball and talking. She put nail polish on me, which I liked, but she also put nail polish on her dog at the same time, which the dog did not appreciate. At puberty we broke off our friendship because she wanted to date and I was not dating material, she preferred boys who were cool "greasers".

In sixth grade, I fell in love with science. I had extra time on my hands because my mother had gone off for a gall bladder operation for six weeks and I was trundled off to my grandparents for weekdays, my father taking care of me during weekends. In my experience, elementary teachers never liked to teach science and never got through more than 20% of science texts during a school year. Having nothing else to do during my stay at my grandparents, I read the sixth grade science text from cover to cover in six weeks. It covered biology, astronomy, chemistry and physics. The behavioral sciences had not yet been incorporated into textbooks. I was still turned on by science in spite of having very little science instruction in elementary school.

In junior high, after homeroom, we had homogenous groupings for academic classes. The more advanced classes were usually pushed a little harder with schoolwork. I again had girlfriends at school but not beyond school time. My mastery of male technologies was less than perfect. I was given a list of things that I needed for gym class that included a jock strap. Not knowing that the purpose of this item was to replace my underwear beneath my short gym shorts, I wore it over my boxers for the first class. My boxers flapped in the breeze from beneath my gym shorts. My gym teacher was amused and I was the subject of ridicule throughout the class. I never made that mistake again.

Strange things began happening in junior high school. Girls started to pull away from me, sharing secrets that I could not know. They went off to a "girls only" health movie in which boys were forbidden. This intrigued me, so by virtue of a bogus bathroom hall pass; I managed to watch through a cracked door. It did not look much different from biology class except that the topic was human biology. I had read all about human biology in the encyclopedia and the science books but this covered details of menstrual periods and pregnancy that did not know.

The girls started growing breasts. This was an experience that I could not share and yet another thing that separated them from me. I remember

Irina who had been placed in a class two years younger than her biological age. She needed extra time to learn English, having recently emigrated from Norway. She had at least an 1-2 year lead of breast development on the other girls and that made her stand out and be the subject of ridicule and wonder. Her genes had also provided her with a full D cup even in junior high school. The boys and some of the girls were constantly giggling about her breasts. I tried to befriend her but she would not talk to me, probably because she was in a constant state of embarrassment but also because she thought I would ridicule her like the others.

I came to realize that it would be hard to ever have friends again. My natural inclination was to make friends with girls but they were now starting to separate from me socially. I did not make friends with boys because they mocked my intelligence and success in school and they knew my mother was a teacher. For the most part I was saved from bullying however because I was still head and shoulders taller and stronger than most boys my age. I began to feel like I could not be a true friend to anyone because I could not reveal that I was crossdressing in private.

Despite feeling like I was in wrong body, I decided to see what the male body would do. I learned how to throw all types of pitches: fastballs, sinkers, sliders and screwballs. I also learned how to be a single wing football center. For those of you unacquainted with the single wing, it was like today's shotgun or wildcat formation except that the job of the center was much more skilled and complicated. I learned the skills from one of my father's employees who had been a single wing center in high school before going off to fight with Patton in Africa. Although this skill was somewhat dated and arcane even at the time I learned it, I used it to good advantage many times later. In junior high school they were still using the single wing so I gave my intramural and all-star teams a competitive advantage. It also later came in handy for high school and college football. Football gave me the opportunity to interact with males but I found it hard to make friends with them particularly in a group situation. One-on-one, I could relate to them but the locker room banter and towel snapping turned me off.

It did not seem that my parents were responsible for the misalignment of my assigned gender with how I felt and behaved. I had spent most of my childhood with my parents, especially my mother but I perceived no ill effects from that. That my parents were actually blamelessness was confirmed when I later started looking in the scientific literature. I learned that there was scientific evidence that my parents had not been responsible in any way for what I later learned are transgenderism or transsexualism.

───────────── ❖ ─────────────

TSTG DEFINITIONS

The emergence of transsexualism (TS) and transgenderism (TG) typically occurs by age 3-4. By transgenderism I mean that there exists an incongruence between the observable gender behavior and/or verbal declarations of an individual and the individual's culturally assigned gender behavior category at birth (usually assigned to be consistent with one's assigned sex). Gender behavior includes dress, makeup and comportment. Male to female (MTF) refers to TSTG who were assigned male at birth but prefer feminine gender behavior. Female to male (FTM) refers to TSTG who were assigned female at birth but prefer masculine gender behavior.

When we are born in most cultures, some medical authority typically declares whether you are male or female. This declaration is usually based on the external genitalia. Each culture has arbitrarily decided what set of gender behaviors go with a babies declared sex. Each child is expected by the culture to learn and adhere to the defined gender behavior category of that sex for the rest of its lives. Some individuals have a predisposition that is inconsistent with their assigned sex and gender behavior category. These individuals may present publicly or privately in the manner of their preferred gender category that is inconsistent with what the culture expects or they may say that they do not fit with their assigned sex and gender category that makes them TSTG. The overt presentation is stronger evidence of TSTG than the verbal declaration but the declaration cannot totally be ignored. Mental health professionals encounter people who say that they are TSTG but on further exploration many are not. That is why they are the gatekeepers of TSTG treatment under the international guidelines of the World Professional Association for Transgender Health (WPATH).

This definition is behavior-oriented and does not rely on any internal intervening variables like "gender identity" because such intervening variables cannot currently be scientifically observed and measured. Maybe someday we will have the technological means to investigate intervening variables, but not now.

Transgender

Transgender (TG) is an umbrella term. Transgenders typically move back and forth between gender behavior categories while transsexuals (TS) typically permanently move to their preferred gender presentation. This usually involves changing their bodies. Transsexuals go through a process called *transition* in which they modify their bodies by taking hormones and hormone blockers, so called *hormone therapy* (HT). They may also undergo various types of surgery including facial feminization surgery, breast implants and genital plastic surgery (GPS).

I have found the acronym TSTG to be useful to refer to the population of both TG and TS. It is still an open to question as to whether the distinction between TS and TG is one of intensity or type but until good evidence appears to indicate a separation I will treat them as one phenomenon. I want to be clear and concise in my writings, and the acronym TSTG works for me. I tend to use it as a noun, plural noun and adjective. Some may object to these usages but I believe that it is better than using a family of circumlocutions that mean the same thing.

Gender Learning

We now know that children grasp the concept of gender by age 2-3 (Serbin, et. al, 2001). They quickly learn the expected presentations and behaviors for each gender behavior category that their culture offers.

Some cultures have more than two gender categories and expected gender behaviors vary between cultures and even subcultures both geographically and historically. For example, in our culture children know the essentials of what color goes with what gender category by age 2, even though the color assignment is purely arbitrary. In fact, before World War I and even up through the late 1940's, pink and blue gender assignments were reversed (Paoletti, 2012). The economic incentive to adopt a color-coding scheme was to sell more clothes. The previous all-white clothing of children was interchangeable between the sexes and color assignment resulted in more sales. This is just one example of the arbitrary nature of gender behavior norms that culture defines but there are many others.

Studies show that TSTG children appear to suffer no deficits in gender learning (Maccoby, 1998; Szkrybalo, 1999; Chiu et al., 2006). They become keen observers of behaviors that they must emulate in order to avoid family and social rejection.

TSTG REALIZATION

The realization that one is TSTG usually occurs when a child is 3-4 years old. At that age, children whose gender predisposition does not match cultural gender expectations associated with their assigned gender category at birth, will discover that they are TSTG, although they may not be able to fully articulate it then. TSTG are encouraged by their parents to conform through gentle persuasion up through severe shaming and punishment. Some are ostracized from the family altogether. Family members and the rest of the culture sometimes support this unethical behavior in order to conform to their cultures. Many children, whose gender predisposition and expected gender behavior do not match, will learn how to pretend to follow the correct gender behavior norms for their assigned sex and keep their true feelings a secret.

Some TSTG experience discomfort in early childhood but cannot understand or articulate what is bothering them until later in life. These "late-bloomers" can suddenly change their gender behavior category to the surprise of their families and friends.

Increasingly, TSTG children are rejecting secrecy about TSTG. Many children who feel very strongly about aligning their predisposition with their behavior and who have understanding parents are now treated respectfully. They may be allowed to completely switch over to the gender presentation with which they are most comfortable. Children are increasingly taking chemical blockers to prevent puberty. At age 16, they can make a decision to transition or not.

GENDER DYSPHORIA

The current clinical buzzword for the TSTG phenomena is called gender dysphoria, literally meaning from the Greek that one is unhappy about their assigned gender behavior category. But the commonly accepted term is that these people are transgender or transsexual. The buzzwords keep changing because there are strong forces in the TSTG and mental health communities to push TSTG out of the category of mental disorders. They just keep changing the clinical terms and moving them around in the taxonomy of medical codes. There will be more about this in Chapter 5.

SUGGESTED PARENTAL CAUSES OF TSTG

TSTG has been attributed to several parental child-rearing mistakes, although the scientific evidence contradicts these suggested TSTG causes. The suggested child-rearing mistakes are:
- Smother mother; distant father
- Mother wanting a different sex child
- Being raised in the wrong gender behavior category.
- Being unable to learn appropriate gender behaviors
- Abuse

SMOTHER MOTHER/DISTANT FATHER

A smother mother is one who attempts to control all of the behaviors of a child. A distant father is one who is not available for gender teaching or emotional support. Studies show that the smother mother/distant father hypothesis is false (Zucker, 1994). Having a smother mother or distant father does not cause TSTG.

At some points in my life I felt like I was smothered by my mother and I did not have much contact with my father. Because of commuting to school by car, I was with her most of my waking moments in elementary and junior high school and nearly as much in high school. A factor in my choice of college was to get as far away from my hometown as possible to be my own person, but there were other factors including the strength of the football programs. And, oh yes, the caliber of academics was a factor. As for my father, we had nothing but a positive relationship although we did not communicate much about emotions. He brought me along on his wildlife management check-up trips, we watched TV together, and we played catch. He came to my football games, even in the pouring rain.

TSTG behavior could conceivably cause a mother to become more protective of her child and a father to become more distant because the child behaves in an unexpected manner. These are the effects of TSTG, not the causes. I can understand, but not excuse, how parents of TSTG reject their children because of ignorance, culture and fear. But I was never rejected. I had successfully kept my secret and was playing the role of a model boy.

Birth Preference

A common suggested theory of TSTG is that one's mother would have preferred that her child to have been of the other sex. This notion was refuted by a study that it was shown that there was no relationship between TSTG and a mother's preferred sex prior to delivery (Zucker, 1994). Mothers cannot make you TSTG because they wanted a child of the opposite sex.

Child Raised in Wrong Gender Category

There have been at least two famous "natural experiments" that bear on this suggested cause. In both of these cases surgical mistakes were made during circumcision resulting in loss of the penis. Follow-up genital plastic surgery was performed to make their outer genitalia look like females. Health care professionals mistakenly told their parents that they would become women if raised that way. Both of these "experiments" resulted in rejection of gender rearing and, in one case, suicide (Reiner, 2004; Bradley et. al, 1998). One of these cases was documented in a best-selling book "As Nature Made Him" (Colopinto, 2000). My experience is that my mother seemed content with having a boy and, if anything, urgently wanted me to be a model boy and man.

GENDER LEARNING DEFICIT

As mentioned earlier, studies show that TSTG children appear to suffer no deficit in gender learning ability (Maccoby, 1998; Szkrybalo, 1999; Chiu et al., 2006). They are not exhibiting TSTG behavior because they do not know the gender norms.

Most TSTG children are well motivated to learn the culturally assigned gender behaviors that are associated with their assigned sex. They are well motivated by the threat of rejection by their families or culture. They become "students of the game" and "role players" and learn these arbitrary behaviors even though they conflict with their gender predispositions. Through practice and correction, many TSTG become very good at the pretending act. In fact many TSTG later have to learn new gender behaviors and "gender craft" that match their predispositions if they decide to improve their presentations or transition. This is because they have insufficient practice and sometimes need an instruction manual (Prince, 1976).

My experience is that I have learned "masculine craft" well enough to survive in the military research world for over 50 years. When I decided to dress in public as a woman for the first few times I had to actually reference a "how-to" manual written by Virginia Prince (Prince, 1979). As a result, at first I dressed entirely in feminine business suits but now I am comfortable presenting in a more relaxed manner.

Childhood Trauma from Abuse

There is no evidence to support the theory that TSTG is due to childhood trauma inflicted by parents, although this theory frequently crops up in the media and from "reparative therapy" practitioners. Reparative therapy practitioners attempt to eliminate TSTG behaviors (and also homosexual behaviors) by using positive and negative reinforcement and other approaches, even though the efficacy of reparative therapy is rejected by all reputable mental health organizations. Indeed, reparative therapy has caused many to be traumatized and should be considered abuse.

My parents certainly never abused me either physically or psychologically and in all my conversations with other TSTG people over the years no one has ever mentioned child abuse causing their TSTG.

———————— ❖ ————————

During childhood I had a nearly overwhelming sense of loneliness. It was partly due to the physical isolation of our family but it was also due to secrecy about my TSTG. I did not blame my parents for my TSTG and I did not blame them when they informed me about the future burden of "becoming a man." My parents, after all, were trying to prepare me for the "grown-up" world I would have to face and probably did not think they had any choice. However, I was just starting to understand that being a man would subject me to intense loneliness.

During childhood, the secrecy and loneliness grew as I gradually began losing all my female friends and not being able to have close male friends. Being constantly on guard against revealing my secret limited my having intimate friends, male or female. I could not candidly talk to anyone for fear that indications of the secret be revealed. I gradually put aside my love of music and art lest these be seen as "feminine". Loneliness was the best word I could find at the time, the word depression not being applied to people outside of mental institutions in that era. The result was that I sampled people rather than engaging them and for the most part stuck to the books, sports and myself.

The psychology on secrecy has established that secrecy frequently leads to loneliness, depression and potential suicide (Kelly, 2002). Loneliness is self-imposed to avoid revealing the secret. Many TSTG suffer from depression. Not from the organic depression which is well publicized and due to an imbalance in brain chemicals. The depression that TSTG typically suffer from is the situational depression that results from their secrecy and/or rejection. The frequency of attempted suicide in TSTG is believed to be around 31-43% (Grant et al., 2010, Mustanski and Liu, 2012) and contributes to suicide in young adults being an especially significant public health problem (and Mustanski, 2001; Mustanski and Liu, 2012).

Blaming TSTG on child rearing seems to be part of a recurring cultural phenomenon. Our culture goes through phases when all manner of problems are attributed to bad parental child rearing skills. The definition of good and bad child rearing skills is constantly changing, so parents are constantly found guilty.

———————— ❖ ————————

Because I was such a good soprano, I was recruited to sing the feature song for my 8th grade graduation. The school retained a local singing coach to help me get ready over the several weeks remaining until the ceremony. Something was going terribly wrong. My enunciation improved from the lessons but my range of low to high notes was measurable decreasing every lesson for some reason. It got so bad that they sent me off to the doctor to have my throat painted with silver nitrate to no avail. I did manage to sing the song at graduation but three weeks later I was a tenor and a month later a baritone. Puberty had hit me without warning and my childhood was at an end.

Chapter 1 References

Bradley, S., Oliver, G., Chernick, A., & Zucker, K. (1998). Experiment of Nurture: Ablatio Penis at 2 Months, Sex Reassignment at 7 Months, and a Psychosexual Follow-up in Young Adulthood. Pediatrics. 102(1), 1-5.

Chiu, S., Gervan, S., Fairbrother, C., Johnson, L., Owen-Anderson A., & Bradley, S. (2006). Sex-Dimorphic Color Preference in Children with Gender. Sex Roles 55, 385–395.

Colopinto, J. (2006). *As Nature Made Him: The Boy Who Was Raised as a Girl.* Harper Perennial.

Grant, J., Mottet, L., Tanis, J., Herman, J., Harrison, J., & Keisling, M. (2010). National Transgender Discrimination Survey Report on Health and Health Care. Findings of a Study by the National Center for Transgender Equality and the National Gay and Lesbian Task Force. October 2010.

Kelly, A. (2002). *The Psychology of Secrets.* New York: Plenum.

Liu R., & Mustanski B. (2001). Suicidal ideation and self-harm in lesbian, gay, bisexual, and transgender youth. American Journal of Preventative Medicine. Mar; 42(3): 221-8.

Maccoby E. (1998). *The Two Sexes Growing Up Apart, Coming Together.* Harvard University Press, Cambridge, MA.

Mustanski B, & Liu R. (2012). A Longitudinal Study of Predictors of Suicide Attempts Among Lesbian, Gay, Bisexual, and Transgender Youth Archives of Sexual Behavior. Oct 5.

Paoletti, J. (2012). Pink and Blue: T*elling the Boys from the Girls in America.* Indiana University Press. Feb 6.

Prince, V. (1976). *Understanding Cross-Dressing.* Los Angeles: Chevalier Publications.

Prince, V. (1979). *How to Be a Woman though Male.* Chevalier Publications, Los Angeles.

Reiner W., & John P Gearhart J. (2004). Discordant Sexual Identity in Some Genetic Males with Cloacal Exstrophy Assigned to Female Sex at Birth. The New England Journal of Medicine. 350(4), 333.

Serbin L., Poulin-Dubois D., Colburne K., Sen M., & Eichstedt J., (2001). Gender stereotyping in infancy: Visual preferences for and knowledge of gender-stereotyped toys in the second year. International Journal of Behavioral Development. 25 (1), 7–15.

Szkrybalo J., & Ruble D. (1999). "God Made Me a Girl": Sex-Category Constancy Judgments and Explanations Revisited. Developmental Psychology, 32(2), 1649.

Uddenberg N., Walinder J., & Hojerback T. (1979) Parental contact in male and female transsexuals. Acta Psychiatrica Scandanavia. 60(1), 113-20.

Zucker K., Green R., Garofano C., Bradley S., Williams K., Rebach H. (1994). Prenatal preferences of mothers of feminine and masculine boys. Journal of Abnormal Child Psychology. 22(1), 1-13.

CHAPTER TWO

High School and Sexual Arousal

Here I am under the goalposts, all alone.
-Poem fragment, 1964

My high school years were dominated by a combination of sexual arousal and loneliness.

I think I had an erection for most of the time in high school. There was no respite, even at night when the wet dreams would come. There were seven reasons for this.

The first reason I was sexually aroused was, of course I had started puberty. Increases in androgen levels including testosterone and growth hormone levels had started before that junior high graduation. While they helped in sports to make me larger and stronger, my growth created an underlying physiological sensitivity. In this regard, I believe I experienced puberty as other males do.

Another reason is that the girls in high school dressed to arouse, whether by conformity or competitiveness. Their novelty and variety was bewildering. This was in the early 60's. Girls captured and displayed every sexual stimulus that I had ever seen in the magazines and on TV and some stimuli I had not seen before. Some who had been my girl friends in elementary school had upgraded their presentations. Some girls were "exotic", coming from the nearby "sending districts" that were too small to have their own high schools and lived in a different subculture. From head to toe they were walking (and sitting) sexual arousal displays. This was the era of the bouffant hairdo but the beehive and the flip and the pageboy were still common. Some girls would put curlers in their hair at night and sleep on them in order to have a perky hairdo the next day. Hair teasing was rampant and the smell of hairspray was constantly in the halls. The girls had also discovered makeup and perfume. It was scary but arousing to see them in blue and green eye shadow. They generally wore tight sweaters or blouses that showed off their breasts. And, of course, there were rumors of breast enhancement inserts, otherwise known as "falsies" from girls that shared the girls' locker room. Skirts were short and tight. Stockings were nearly mandatory except when the weather really got hot. Heels were high and clicky. All these stimuli were novel to me and triggered intense and persistent arousal. I am sure that my cohort males going through puberty experienced arousal from these females. The arousal was distracting and interfered with my social interactions with former or potential girl friends.

The third reason that I was erect all the time was that the classes were again assigned homogenously, with the better students in the top classes. And the better students at this age were still mainly girls and a few of us males. There was no respite in class for me.

Reason number four was that I was curious about how girls presented themselves and how they behaved, since I knew that deep down inside I was a girl. Someday I thought I would be able to become one of them. So I paid meticulous attention to their dress, makeup and behavior. Of course, observing their presentation details also caused sexual arousal. The sexual arousal was not directed at the girls per se, it was the novelty of their presentation details. I am sure that non-TSTG heterosexual males did not pay as close attention to females or experience them in the same way I did.

Reason number five is that I masturbated every opportunity I had and invented new opportunities. I would go to my unheated bedroom to pretend that I was studying and would put on my mother's discarded thigh-hi stockings under the covers and wore lipstick. I could hear my parents if they came up the stairs and take off the lipstick. Since it was cold, I could cover my legs without too much suspicion. Masturbation brought relief but my refractory period when I could not get erect seemed like only a few minutes.

Reason number six is that I was now partially cross-dressing under my clothing much of the time. My mother's girdles and panties were a source of arousal as well as protection from the bulges of erections that were becoming increasingly obvious. I would sit in homeroom in the morning, daydreaming and get erect. When the bell rang for first period, this required me to put my briefcase in front of my crotch as I walked down the hall. I later found that holding my breath would reduce the erections but that was impractical much of the time.

The seventh reason that I was aroused much of the time was that there were dominant girls who must have sensed that I could be put in constant arousal and made the most of it. These girls had no formal training in BDSM (bondage, discipline, sadism, masochism), unlike some women who I was to meet later in life. They just seemed to come by it naturally and were probably experimenting. Some of these girls seemed to look through me and know immediately about my feminine, submissive side. They would exploit this perception by trying to drive me crazy with arousal. At which point I would do anything they asked.

This dominance/submission game actually started on the first week of school in which freshman had to wear a big sandwich-board sign announcing their underclass status. Hazing was allowed and I got my share of blue eye shadow and lipstick and wearing sexy lingerie over my clothes while changing classes. This type of hazing continued a few months later at the annual Latin club banquet in which freshmen were sold off for service for the night during a "slave auction." Such and event would certainly not be politically correct today for all kinds of reasons. And of course my buyer was an older female cousin who had a BDSM streak in her. On went the lipstick and the eye shadow, in went the pacifier and on went the sexy dress. It must have been her mother's dress in order to fit my big frame.

Once in class, these dominant girls would tease me in class by rubbing my elbow or back from an adjacent desk. One would put perfume on me when my back was turned or pass me a note that said "Smile if you are wearing a red bra." They would invite me to sit next to them in class or assembly and I could not dare to refuse. They would call me up and invite me on dates, like church hayrides, church retreats or the Sadie Hawkins dance. They were in charge. Post event activities would include having me caress them for long periods of time. This drove me crazy. One had a habit of requiring me to stand at the bottom of the stairs while we were both fully clothed so she could mount my erection. Sometimes the girls would just stop what they were doing and leave me in a puddle on the floor.

I suppose most males would have regarded being treated this way by high school girls as an invitation for sexual conquest but I was not one of them. Aside from the sexual arousal, I actually enjoyed the feminine attention.

❖

High school meant that I had access to some better reference and biology books in the school library. But what I learned made me concerned that I might be dressing up in feminine clothing and makeup just for a "cheap sexual thrill." Not that I minded some cheap sexual thrills, but it created confusion between my confused my desire to be a woman and my enjoyment of sexual arousal.

The encyclopedia and library told me that a "*transvestite*" was someone who crossdressed and behaved like the opposite sex for the purpose of sexual arousal. More precisely that, for the purpose of sexual arousal, they temporarily acted in the opposite gender behavior category to which they had been assigned at birth. The word "transvestite" is simply derived from Latin meaning "crossdressing." However, from its coinage by Magnus Hershfeld, an early German sexologist, the word has had the connotation of sexual arousal. For a long time transvestism was used as a term indicating a sexual fetish and pathological behavior disorder. It was later replaced by the English "crossdressing" as a more neutral term in the latter half of the twentieth century. The term crossdressing was used to apply to the behavior and not to its motivation.

For sure I was crossdressing and for sure I was sexually aroused by it and so I fit the description of a transvestite. I was not primarily crossdressing to become sexual aroused, I wanted to be a girl and wanted to see what it was like. Sexual arousal was a side benefit.

I was still afraid of being committed to a mental hospital as I saw another of our neighbors being hauled away. This time it was the brother of the first neighbor girl. The word schizophrenia was used in conjunction with these commitments but I was not really sure what that was from the reference book descriptions.

And I now had another reason to be secretive. I now even knew the name of my "mental illness" and it was "transvestic fetishism."

❖

There is a public perception, and actually still held by some scientists that the motivation for TSTG is sexual arousal and therefore its underlying cause. And what do we know about sexual arousal and TSTG? Does it help us explain TSTG causation? Do TSTG just crossdress for a fetish or "cheap thrills." If sexual arousal is not the motivation for TSTG, how does one separate the motivations for sexual arousal from the motivations to practice TSTG behavior? What do we know about sexual arousal, anyway? It took a long time for me to find out because most of the science had not yet begun when I was a child.

First we know that the development of sexual arousal starts in childhood (Walter and Buyske, 2003; Weingart et. al., 1998; Wolf, 1995) and does not get into high gear until adolescence and early adulthood. Presumably the function of sexual arousal is to get sex organs ready for sexual behavior that is important for continuing the species. Genital secretions start flowing and erections begin.

The physiological foundation for sexual arousal is the presence of androgens and estrogens that rises dramatically in puberty. These hormones result in growth of genitalia, breasts and hair. They also prime the body to respond to sexual stimuli, indeed spontaneous erections occur in waking males and "wet dreams" including erections and orgasm occur at night during sleep.

Novel stimuli are the best stimuli at triggering male sexual arousal. We know that novelty can trigger sexual arousal from the work of Frank Beach (Ford and Beach, 1952) who performed extensive work with animals. Beach's experimentation showed that the presence of a new female dog triggered sexual arousal even in male dogs that had just mated with another female. Novel and new stimuli, particularly those associated with the opposite sex can trigger sexual arousal.

We know that sexual arousal to a particular stimulus can be learned by repeated pairing of a neutral stimulus with sexual arousal (Hoffmann, H., Jansson E., Turner S.L., 2004). The learning mechanism is called Classical or Pavlovian Conditioning. In this form of learning, a previously arbitrary neutral stimulus, in this case some aspect of feminine or masculine presentation is paired with sexual arousal. When this pairing occurs, the body later reacts to the neutral stimulus by causing sexual arousal. If the stimulus is novel, the learning proceeds even faster.

The phenomenal of Classical Conditioning has been exhaustively studied, so its principles of operation are well understood. It has been around since Pavlov at the turn of the last century who conditioned dogs in the laboratory to salivate when they heard a bell. The first principle, the principle of *acquisition,* is that repeated pairings, close in time, of a stimulus and a physiological reaction strengthen the learned response. Stimulus novelty increases the likelihood of acquisition and response. A second principle, that of *extinction* or *desensitization* is that the same stimulus, if presented and not paired with sexual arousal, will decrease in response strength.

Desensitization or extinction is so well understood that it is used in therapy. It is used in therapeutic desensitization to relieve a patient of unreasonable emotions. For example, fears, say of heights, spiders or Iraq in the case of posttraumatic stress responses. The patient is taught how to relax and is gradually exposed to more intense stimuli until the stimuli do not have any effect.

If sexual arousal is provoked by novelty and follows Pavlovian conditioning principles, then repeated TSTG crossdressing should extinguish or cause desensitization and reduce the strength of the arousal response. At first TSTG are aroused by their experiences with opposite gender category presentation involving clothing or makeup or behavior. No doubt that these experiences are pleasurable. As the stimulus novelty and conditioning wear off, the potential for a stimulus to provoke sexual arousal is reduced. Those who continue to perform TSTG behavior then must be doing it for reasons other than sexual arousal. And indeed there are reports that this is true (Prince, 1976).

Long term, TSTG behave as they do because there is an incongruity between their culturally assigned gender behavior category (culturally associated with birth sex), and their gender behavior predispositions. In my experience, I can report that I have experienced a reduction in sexual arousal to the trappings of crossdressing from TSTG behavior. Even back in high school, I noticed that wearing the nylons in bed was no longer of interest and remembering the hazing scenes no longer were arousing. To this day I do get a thrill out of wearing new and novel feminine clothing but this fades in a matter of minutes. In the long run, sexual arousal can be ruled out as a sustaining cause of TSTG.

Sexual arousal learning principles are also demonstrated in BDSM (bondage, discipline, sadism, masochism) behavior, feminine fashion and pornography wherein old stimuli are replaced by newer, novel stimuli to provoke sexual and emotional arousal.

As carried out by knowledgeable (and usually safe) practitioners of BDSM in support group clubs, the career of BDSM practitioners follows a predictable pattern due to the principles of novelty and Classical Conditioning extinction. The usual progression is to start as a submissive who trusts themselves to one or more dominants to experience stimuli and situations which are, at first, frightening and sexually arousing (e.g. being tied up, flogging, mummification, weak electrical stimulation.) As desensitization occurs and novelty fades these "scenes" lose their sexual arousal capability. They players then have to move to a new set of stimuli, sometimes more painful or frightening/intense. Through desensitization players experience more intense stimuli which would not have been tolerated initially. When submissives have experienced all of the stimuli included in the accepted club "scenes", they often become dominants and use their experience to play with new submissives.

Women's fashions follow a pattern of trying to find new looks and stimuli that will provoke sexual arousal and artistic emotion. The stimuli lose their novelty quickly and are again replaced with newer ones. Periodically, designs and stimuli are recycled after a period of absence with small tweaks that make them novel again.

Response to pornography also follows Classical Conditioning learning rules regarding sexual arousal. The sexual arousal that pornographic stimuli provoke also extinguishes with repeated presentation. New and/or more intense stimuli replace the old ones until those are also exhausted. The result is search for novel stimuli, sometimes into harder core niches.

In our culture, women have nearly complete control over the presentation of novel stimuli that can provoke sexual arousal. Men are traditionally confined to boring fabrics and clothing and few cosmetics. Men are encouraged not to make a lot of effort on their appearance. Males that display any of these feminine stimuli are judged as having crossed the gender category line and are defined as effeminate. For females crossing the gender category line is tolerated in most western cultures. In other cultures and times, men were expected to grow their hair long, dress in frilly clothing or wear high heels (the concept of red soled high heel soles was borrowed by the current designer Christian Laboutin from the fashion of males in the French Court of Louis XIV).

There are occasional male revolts against the cultural rules. One of interest is the "metrosexual." A metrosexual is a male or female that takes particular care of their grooming and appearance and may marginally violate some of the gender rules. Another recurring revolt involves skirts for men, and at last check, there were about a half a dozen designers offering them, more than ever before. Male models, like Andrej Pejic now rule the female clothing runways and this trend has significantly increased in recent years. We will see whether these revolts have permanent results or fade away as many revolts have done.

Drag queens and Kings know exactly what stimuli are sexually arousing and exaggerate them for fun and/or for theater. Conventionally a drag queen is supposed to be a gay male but "drag queen behavior" is an equal opportunity activity. There are gay and straight, male and female drag queens. More germane to the issue of gender behavior, there are TSTG and non-TSTG drag queens and kings. Although they may perform or dress up in another gender category "on stage", how they dress and present themselves "off stage" may be totally different.

———————— ❖ ————————

Aside from nearly constant sexual arousal, I also remember the abject loneliness of high school. The loneliness resulted from my secret that I was really a woman. Along with sexual arousal it interfered with relationships with females. By itself it interfered with male relationships. I called it loneliness then but today we might call it situational depression.

Keeping a secret can have adverse effects on both health and relationships. Keeping a secret is stressful and has been associated with situational depression, anxiety, pain and vulnerability to infectious diseases (Kelly, 2002). Remembering what information constitutes a secret creates an endless loop of thinking and calculating how to keep the secret through denial and/or deception. In order to avoid the burden of thinking and calculating and being deceitful people often withdraw, resulting in loneliness. As in my childhood, my strategy was to withdraw from potential friends. Since I did not live in the city, I could retreat to the country every night after school activities. And I tried to compartmentalize my school contacts so that I did not have to get too close to any one classmate.

The loneliness got so bad that I wrote a poem about it. My English teacher and faculty high school newspaper overseer actually liked it. This was unusual because, in general, I avoided English composition and poetry writing because of potential leaks in secret keeping. (I stopped doing art in the eighth grade for the same reason.) Writing inevitably made what was implicit and hidden in my nervous system into something explicit. I have long since lost the poem but it was about being on the football field at night, after a game had been played and here I was "under the goal posts, alone." My English teacher liked my poem so much that she published it in the high school newspaper. I could not tell whether she actually thought the poem was good English literature or whether she thought it was just a typical expression from a naïve adolescent.

Publishing the poem was a temporary catastrophe for me. First my classmates and then my football coach piled on the criticism. The coach said that it dripped with sentimentalism and was the worst literature he had ever read. (At least he called it literature). I guess he saw sentimentality as antithetical to the violent emotions that football required. I never wrote another poem again.

If there was a good thing about the loneliness poem, it was that the football coach found out from my English teacher that I had good grades. As part of the lonely withdrawal strategy, I had carefully compartmented my football playing from my academics for fear of ridicule from either compartment. I also feared that one side or the other would have enough information to suspect my secret. (Later when I worked in the military and intelligence communities, the concept of information compartmentalization was already intuitively known to me.) The coach's knowledge that I had good grades led to his advocacy for scholar-athlete awards and for getting me recruited by elite colleges to play football. I am sure that he did this to be helpful to me but also because he could claim a victory on his resume for getting one of his players into a prestigious school.

My unsuccessful friendships with girls made me feel especially rejected and lonely. As I related previously, I was sexually aroused by the stimuli that girls displayed. The arousal interfered with trying to converse or be around them. However, the girls clearly did not regard me as a potential suitor even though I was a male and clearly was sexually aroused. Being on the football team gave me no standing to be a suitor for some reason. When we were talking academics things seemed a little different. But talking about math or science was not conducive to close friendships, either. Occasionally, one of the girls would talk to me one-on-one and I made some progress, but when we were in a group, I was just another male and not one desirable as a suitor.

The loneliness I felt and all TSTG feel is a form of situational depression that is unrelated to the "organic" depression that we now can treat with mood enhancing drugs. Organic depression is a long-term neurotransmitter problem. Situational or reactive depression is depression resulting from events and situations that is a perfectly normal human response to the situation. In the TSTG situation the loneliness and depression that we feel is in reaction to having to keep a secret, not fitting in with peers, and avoiding social situations because they are painful. The loneliness is to some extent self-inflicted by deliberate separation from people. We are lonely because we chose to be alone.

I did have a few dates early in high school but that was also awkward because I wanted a pal, rather than a romantic or sexual relationship. I spent most of my time during dates, putting myself in their places and thinking about how it must be for them. Of course, this was a distraction from actually relating to my date. I tried to be appropriately sexually aggressive but it was not in my nature and I was bad at it.

Later in high school I did get adopted by a group of girls and boys who were two years younger than me. I got passed around from girl to girl but one, in particular, stuck with me as a friend and lover. Our relationship gradually ended as I sensed she was getting too close. It was a lost opportunity.

Girls now had their own groups and I was disqualified by sex. They spent time with each other in clubs and with each other. I could not compete with this. My attempt at friendships I had with girls in high school must have had some effect as indicated at my class reunion. Much to the confusion of my wife at the time, when the girls in my class discovered that I was at the reunion, they assembled around me and were all excited and giggling. My wife saw it as them recalling me as a handsome, virile, high school football hero which filled her with jealousy. I saw it as an expression that, at least to some extent, I had gained a little acceptance as one of the girls.

I had no close male friends, because I feared reveling my TSTG secret and feminine predisposition and because everything boys did repulsed me anyway. In addition to having classes with some boys (the academic group), I also was out for football and spent time with a different group of raucous football players. The academic boys were okay with a few exceptions. I also did not have to see them naked. Some were not really interested in academics and complained about how hard the work was. Some were better than I was at engineering-related areas. None of them were particularly obnoxious but I had no close male friends in this group.

On the other hand, the football group was particular obnoxious and that was just the way our coached liked them, full of piss and vinegar. Locker rooms were filled with towel snapping, grab ass and wrestling matches, none of which I engaged in.

On the field my teammates liked defense because they could beat hell out of the opposing players and create mischief. On offense it was sometimes hard for my teammates to get organized. I tried to call the blocking patterns from my position as center but my teammates did not always do what they were supposed to do. Our most successful play was for me to direct snap the ball to our tailback that gave him the option of passing or running. I could lead him one way or the other which gave him a few steps advantage. He could throw the ball about 65 yards from scrimmage. It was hard to find teammates who could actually catch the ball at that distance but the effect was that it stretched out the defenders for his running. His Howdy Doody running style was awkward but effective as he scrambled out of the backfield. When we were facing a team that used the single wing formation, I had to practice against the varsity defense, rather than with them. I was so glad when football season was over. While I enjoyed the intellectual part of the game, I was grossed out by the boys and happy every time I got through a season without injury.

Ironically, I got some respite from the sexual arousal and loneliness of high school because of Sputnik. Sputnik also set me on a career path towards the social sciences and away from medicine and engineering. Sputnik was the first orbiting satellite. It was launched by the Russians a few months before the US could launch one of our own. It set the US military community in a tizzy because it meant to some that the Russians had a lead in space and missiles. Space was a new battlefield for the Cold War. Satellites were needed for reconnaissance; missiles that traveled through space were needed to attack at intercontinental distances. Because of our failures to be the first in space, it was felt that our math and engineering capabilities were lacking. Improving them became a national priority and educational enrichment programs were started. In one of the educational programs, the National Science Foundation sent promising students to college for an 8-week camp where they would learn from professors in engineering, science and computer science. With the recommendations of my teachers I was selected to go to one of these camps, much to my parents patriotic approval. It prevented me from earning any money that summer but duty called.

The camp was all male and held at an all-male college in the boondocks of upper New England. I tolerated the math, chemistry, physics and math courses but I really loved the course entitled "Science and the Social Sciences." where we read C.P. Snow's book about the rift between science and the social sciences. We also wrestled with issues such as the ethical responsibilities of scientists to prevent use of the atomic bomb after they had developing it. That summer I also got into the greatest physical shape of my life. There wasn't any homework, and the northern sun did not set until almost 10. So, after dinner I would play soccer for several hours. The boys at the camp were less athletic but more tolerable than the ones back at home on the football team. When we started fall football practice and my coach saw me make a good defensive play, my coach asked what I had done all summer. Had I been eating nails?

By the time I got to my senior prom, I foolishly did not invite the only girl with whom I had a close relationship who was two years behind me. Instead I chose a girl in my class whom I thought was safe but whom I really did not know. At the prom, I had had enough. As was the custom, I was supposed to take my date to the beach the next day, but I stood her up on the beach trip because I just needed to be alone.

My football coach had been successful in getting me an award as a scholar-athlete in my senior year, even though I had broken my hand and missed half the games. He also succeeded in getting the attention of top academic college coaches who literally came to my door to recruit me.

I was also invited to visit each of the schools and picked out a far away all-male school that had the best football team and the opportunity for me to get into Army ROTC that would allow me to complete college without being drafted. I had opted to go it alone and to seek the most physically risky course. I never thought that my parents were to blame for my TSTG situation, but I wanted to be on my own. I also did not want to be continually tortured by women who sexually aroused me when what I really wanted was friendship. I wanted activities that required me to concentrate, like sports and military operations. I also saw this as a path to manhood, but I was mistaken.

Chapter 2 References

Ford, C. & Beach, F. (1951). *Patterns of Sexual Behavior*. New York: Harper & Row.

Hoffmann, H., Jansson E., & Turner S. (2004). Classical Conditioning of Sexual Arousal in Women and Men: Effects of Varying Awareness and Biological Relevance of the Conditioned Stimulus. Archives of Sexual Behavior. 33(1), 43–53.

Kelly, A. (2002). *The Psychology of Secrets*. New York: Plenum.

Prince, V. (1976). *Understanding Cross-Dressing*. Los Angeles: Chevalier Publication.

Walter, A., & Buyske, S. (2003). The Westermarck Effect and early childhood co-socialization: Sex differences in inbreeding-avoidance. British Journal of Developmental Psychology. 21(3), 353-365.

Weingart et al. (eds.) (1998). "*Human By Nature.*" Mahwah, Lawrence Erlbaum.

Wolf, A. (1995). *Sexual attraction and childhood association: A Chinese brief for Westermarck*. Stanford, CA: Stanford University Press.

CHAPTER THREE

College and Terminology

They made him a second lieutenant
And pinned those gold bars on his chest.
They made him a forward observer
And soon had to lay him to rest
ROTC, ROTC, it sounds like some bull* to me, to me.
ROTC, ROTC, it sounds like some bull* to me, to me.
-The ROTC Song sung to the tune of My Bonnie Lies Over the
Ocean

When I use a word,' Humpty Dumpty said, in rather a scornful
tone, 'it means just what I choose it to mean neither more nor less.'
-Lewis Carroll

When I make a word do a lot of work like that,' said Humpty
Dumpty, 'I always pay it extra.'
-Lewis Carroll

I had a new beginning at a far away all-male college with plenty of exciting and dangerous manly things to do. I was expecting to make new male friends. I was expecting to "find myself." I did find an interest in psychology that persists today. My psychology courses gave me better understanding of TSTG. But things did not turn out as I expected in other areas.

It is quiet typical for MTF TSTG to take on risky, physical, dangerous activities and occupations (Brown, 1988). There seem to be a disproportionate number of TSTG soldiers, firemen, and policemen. These jobs are preferable to expressing MTF TSTG and risking cultural rejection. They provide perfect cover stories for hiding TSTG. No one would ever suspect that a he-man military officers or first responders could be TSTG.

And saving the world or at least a part of it gives TSTGs a purpose for living. Because these occupations require intense mental concentration, they can take one's mind off TSTG, providing at least temporary relief.

I had set college up as a test of manhood by enrolling in mountain and winter ROTC, and playing intercollegiate football. I did not completely succeed at either activity but learned a lot about myself in the process.

I found almost immediately that I was not cut out to be the kind of military leader for which the ROTC instructors were looking. Just as in football, military operations became an intellectual game. I was not a natural prancing military leader on the drill field with a "command voice." We took turns commanding close order drill. After trying me out a few times, I became the least preferred drill sergeant. I did not have the requisite military bearing, and preferred to smile rather than exhibit the military grimace.

I spent as little time as possible in the ROTC offices. The hard-core cadets spent lots of time sucking up to the ROTC training officers who were experienced soldiers. I refused to do that, preferring to spend time on my studies. My shoes and buckles were often not shined to perfection because I really did not know how to do it. There were tricky ways of getting the good boot shine by using a candle, which I never mastered.

Just as I was a good student of the masculine game, I was a good student of the military game. I learned the technologies and the tricks of military strategy and tactics. In sophomore year, because a required course for my major conflicted with the watered down ROTC military history course, I ended up in the "real" military history course. The real military history course was taught by the same instructor but populated with upper class history majors. Instead of being the easier cadet course which featured "a battle a day", it was a course on what really mattered in military strategy and organization. A former pentagon historian taught the course. He had particular expertise on the decision to drop the A-bomb in World War II. He emphasized the research and development of logistics and military technology. He portrayed these military elements as the most salient deciding factors in may wars. I loved the course and got one of my first A's from it.

I was a decent skier for mountain and winter warfare. During the winter months, I skied nearly everyday, either for ROTC or physical education. (Yes, back then colleges still had required physical education). I frequently enraged the ski instructors because I did not ski the "Austrian way." The ski instructors in my ROTC detachment were from Austria and they exclusively taught the Austrian military ski technique. To me it did not seem very graceful. Instead of down-up-down with my knees on the turns I did up-down-up on the turns. I found out later that this was how some world-class French and some Canadians skied and is perfect acceptable to everyone else but the Austrians. The whole idea was to unweight the skis, so that they would turn easier and that could be done both ways.

I already was a decent marksman. However, I was at first mystified that I did not make it onto the rifle team. I found out as a result of this failure that I was beginning to get nearsighted even as a freshman in college. I ended up getting ROTC glasses, the black plastic military frames that were popular at the time. The glasses shattered just before rifle qualification testing. I must have been a pretty good marksman after all, because even with shattered lenses taped together, I actually got my marksmanship badge and certification on the M14 rifle at 300 yards.

I passed the one ROTC for-credit course that mainly consisted of how to capture bigger and bigger hills with bigger and bigger military units, starting with the squad and ending with the division. Because I knew the technologies, I excelled on weapons placement and writing the operations plan. Got an A in that one, too.

Between junior and senior year, ROTC sends you to summer camp at a real military base for training by instructors with a wider range of skills and recent combat experience. In this era they were just back from the jungles and rice patties of Vietnam. This was a rite of passage, not unlike boot camp and we would be graded on our performance. It was structured to be physically and mentally stressful with the usual military harassment that I quickly learned how to avoid. Much to my excitement, we got to shoot just about every weapon in the US Army inventory at the time. Just as I had with my father, I carefully studied how each weapon worked and how to operate them. And my father had a menagerie of rifles, shotguns and weapons because he was a game warden. Outlaw hunters in the game preserve discarded most of them just as they were being arrested. Hunting in the fields for weapons after arrests and figuring out how the guns worked became great, good fun.

The 105 recoilless rifle was the most fun and also the scariest. It was not a rifle at all, but a rocket launcher on a jeep. To operate it you would pull out a knob to fire a 50-caliber machine gun with tracers to spot the target, which was the most powerful machine gun in the inventory. Then you would push the knob in to fire the weapon. We lined up with 10 weapons point down range and mine was the last to fire. The first one went off with a whoosh and each succeeding 105 was a little louder and by the time the one before me went off, I realized how powerful a weapon it was. I concentrated on the task anyway, knowing my weapon would rock me. I managed to be the only cadet that actually hit anything that day and with one shot had demolished a derelict armored personnel carrier. I failed miserably at summer camp command exercises but it turned out that our final grade depended mostly on a 500 item multiple choice test which covered all six weeks of the lessons and practical exercises. The test was easy for me and I got one of the highest grades.

I returned to school my senior year, having gotten two A's in the ROTC courses and outscoring everyone in the unit on the summer camp exam. I was clearly in position to be the leader of the cadet corps. I just did not have the predisposition to command, or so the ROTC officer instructors judged. However, they had to do something with me. The consolation prize was to be on the cadet commander's staff and essentially act as the treasurer for unit dues and arranging the military ball and picnics. All I had to do was show up once a week in uniform and shuffle some paper and that was fine with me.

ROTC did not prove my manhood; instead it showed up my technical talents in military science and technology. These would be useful later because I would ultimately make my living doing military research and development and have done so for about 35 years. I knew all the book-learning about how one was supposed to command and act like a military leader but my heart was not in it.

My second adventure into manhood was to go out for college football. Freshman football was a zoo. Approximately 125 students went out for it. This represented about 15% of the freshman class. I was in pretty good shape from running but discovered immediately that I was lacking in upper body strength. I rapidly determined that this college football program was an intellectual step backwards from high school ball. Their practice equipment was similar to what I had used in junior high school. They used outdated, dangerous and ineffective techniques and tactics. They taught to use one's helmet as a battering ram when blocking or tackling, increasing the likelihood of a concussion (this technique is now banned). There were no mouth guards provided, although I still had one from high school. No water was provided during practice. They practiced a technique called a "chop block" in which the first blocker would lift the defender up and the second would go for his knees in an effort to injure. The chop block is now illegal at all levels.

Lineman techniques were primitive compared to what I had learned in high school. The blocking patterns were called by the tackles at the line and as a center, I had nothing do but get rid of the ball. The primary job of defensive lineman was to get in the way of offensive lineman trying to block the linebackers. We were never allowed to penetrate into the backfield to disrupt the play. We were "sacrificial lambs" as a colleague termed it. Things would not get better on the varsity team.

I learned all of the plays and defensive schemes pretty quickly and the coaches learned that I was the best single wing center that they had, in fact, the only one. For the most part, this skill was irrelevant except when we played one particular college team who still ran the single wing and it was one of the last to do so in the college ranks. They ran the single wing primarily to confuse the opposition who had to use up a lot of practice time in preparation for dealing with this antiquated offensive system.

So at the end of freshman football season, I was invited to stay out and play with the varsity. They had one game left and it was with only team in the league that still ran the single wing. They needed someone who could act as a single wing center to help simulate the single wing in practice. I was practicing with the big boys on the varsity team. I watched the films of the opposition and recognized immediately the single wing plays they were running and I knew the subtleties of how to run them. Aside from the single wing, their biggest offensive weapon was an Austrian who became one of the first soccer-style kickers in college and the pros. Clearly they wanted to nullify this kicker who could kick field goals from ungodly ranges. All the opposition needed to do was to get to the opponent 30 and they had a pretty sure 3 points. On kickoffs, the Austrian could put the ball into the end zone with regularity.

I attended the varsity meetings and clearly they were pleased with their progress in combatting the single wing through their practices. However, I found out a somewhat unethical strategy that they planned to use on the soccer-style kicker. They planned to rough him up on the kickoffs by assigning two men to block him, regardless of where the play went. He usually ran directly to the sideline after kicking because he had no knowledge whatsoever about American football blocking and tackling. They were going to use the "hamburger drill" on him in the hopes that he would get injured or at least be timid. The idea of this drill is for one player to knock down an opponent and as soon as the opponent tried to get up, the other player would knock down the opponent. I knew from studying the rulebook that it was technically illegal to hit a player who was clearly not involved in the play and moving away from the play. I guess they figured they could get away with it because the officiating crew would be focused on where the ball was going, rather than pay attention to the kicker. I do not know whether this strategy was effective but I saw the panic of the kicker in the films as he saw two men coming after him. It only appeared in the game films for a few brief seconds before the camera panned to the ball.

During preparation for the single wing team, the weather turned bad for practice and the varsity and I went into the field house that was barren except for a dirt floor. By then I knew the field house well because ROTC used it for close order drill and formations. Practice against the single wing was going well and I was the snapper. All of a sudden, the coaches stopped practice and said that they were going to kick field goals that I thought was odd because there were no goalposts. But I certainly knew how to snap the ball to the holder and then how to deal with the pummeling the center usually took after snapping in order for the defense to try getting into the backfield and blocking the field goal. I snapped the ball, expected a big varsity pummeling, using my best offensive move that was to hit the person across from me as hard as I could. Since my heads was down during the snap, I usually did this almost blindly. To my surprise the defender across from me, did not hit me and was partially crouched over and braced by players laterally on either side. The middle player was having a hard time because I had hit him in his exposed midsection and he was groaning. The whistle blew immediately and I was instructed to snap the ball but not to hit this strange formation. The next play, I snapped the ball and looked up to see the safety sail over me. He had run several yards to a person on all fours put one foot on the players back and jumped to put his next foot on the back of the player across from me. They were going to try to block the soccer style kickers kicks by launching the safety into the air! I went home that night and found that there was no prohibition on what they planned to do. During the game, on the first field goal try by the opposition, the safety was early and onside but the soccer-style kicker had seen his career dissolve before his eyes. On the second attempt at a field goal, the safety was late but the kicker missed badly undoubtedly distracted by the carnival scene in front of him. To make a long story short, the Austrian kicker never scored a field goal on us and we won the game. The varsity team won the trophy for the best college team in the East. The NCAA immediately changed the rules to prohibit this type of defensive kick blocking play.

I guess the coaches thought that I was handy to have around, so they invited me to varsity summer practice camp for the next three years. I was no stronger because I refused to lift weights, spurning weight lifting because of the masculine muscles in the weight room. I was happy enough to run but that was not enough to break into the starting lineup. I finally learned that there was a de facto two-tiered system on the varsity. The upper tier consisted of players that they had carefully recruited as the players that they intended to start. The second tier were players who they needed for practice purposes. They were not likely to move up to the starting tier because the number of live practice plays was severely limited to prevent injury to the first-tier players. There was no way to move up by gaining experience and showing your skill. I finally came to the conclusion that I was playing football for no good reason. I was thoroughly disgusted with the dangerous and illegal techniques that the coaches taught. I suddenly realized that I no longer had to prove anything to anyone. And in my senior year, I left football summer camp to try to secure a place in graduate school.

❖

As in high school, intense loneliness came over me in freshman year and I was at sea. I did not have to suffer from the arousal created by women but I also did not get to enjoy their company at all. The college was all male and isolated, the Interstate road network being incomplete at that time. I decided that I hated males and masculine things. And most importantly, I had no outlet to dress the way I wanted. My grades initially languished because many of my fellow students had already taken college-level courses, sometimes using the same textbook, in prep schools or advanced high schools. My classmates could coast along but I needed a lot of study time to catch up. I went through history, math, international politics, and chemistry without finding something that excited me.

Finally I took introductory psychology at the end of freshman year and things started to click. It was my first A. It offered some insights into human behavior that I was desperate to understand, especially my own. Just as in high school when I was in NSF summer camp, the behavioral sciences became my passion. It was not that the physical sciences were hard but that psychology seemed harder, having to deal with not just biology but also social systems. I became a psychology major at the beginning of sophomore year. Starting with experimental design and statistics, and then on to personality and learning.

Abnormal Psychology was a required course for the major. This course taught that I was a rare freak of nature with a "behavior disorder." Crossdressers, or as they then called TSTG, fetish transvestites were grouped with such "disorders" as homosexuality, fetishism, frottage, exhibitionism, voyeurism and sadomasochism and many other pathological categories. (In 1974, homosexuality was removed from the list of behavior disorders but not TSTG.) Statistics on the frequency of these disorders was not provided by the instructor, so it was up to the student to figure out what "rare" meant. The instructor also was a Freudian and we were required to make Freudian conclusions from case-history descriptions that to me were useless. We learned all about Freudian Oedipus complex, reaction formation and other psychodynamics. In a previous course on personality, the instructor had thoroughly demolished Freudian and psychodynamic theory because it was not a real scientific theory at all and predicted all outcomes.

I was a rare freak of nature with a rare behavior "disorder" and a "fetishistic transvestite." When I had read about Christine Jorgenson and talked to my mother about becoming a woman instead of a man, it seemed as though there must be lots of TSTG out there. My hopes of talking to someone who was TSTG about someday changing my sex became impossible.

Turns out none of the Abnormal Psychology gobbledygook was scientifically correct. First of all, TSTG is not that uncommon. The best estimates that I can obtain from the current literature is that the population frequency of MTF TS is at least .1% (and maybe .2%) of the male population and about half that for FTM. My estimate of TG is that at least 1% (and maybe 2-3%) of males are MTF and, again about half of that frequency for FTM.

My estimates are based on several studies but primarily on the estimates of Conway (Conway, 2001, 2002, Conway and Olyslager, 2007). Lynn Conway is a computer engineer, a Member of the National Academy of Engineering and also a transsexual. She made great strides in chip design that provide the technical basis for modern computers. Her technological advances were not initially celebrated because she was a transsexual woman and her employers thought that she should keep a low profile.

Lynn Conway's TSTG population estimates have been largely ignored by TSTG researchers because of academic and clinical compartmentalization and possibly from other reasons. This ignorance has led to scientific conclusions that are incorrect in many TSTG studies. She used a classic mathematical engineering approach to estimate the frequency in the population of TSTG. She did not count the TSTG coming into a mental health clinic but instead estimated TSTG based on support group membership and the rate of surgeries for TS. This was much more accurate because most TSTG never see a doctor or other mental health professional about their TSTG and are perfectly happy not to do so. Those TSTG who do come to mental health professionals are there mostly to deal with family or cultural rejection issues or TS who want to transition. This is the mathematically correct methodology for making such population estimates but TSTG researchers have largely ignored these studies until recently.

Recent surveys for the UK Health Service to predict TSTG treatment capacity (Reed, et al., 2009) and other studies support Conway's estimates. A recent survey (Kuyper, 2012) in the Netherlands indicates that 4.6% of males and 3.2% of females express dissatisfaction with their assigned gender. This survey probably provides an upper bound on the population frequency of TSTG, since they just asked the question and did not actually observe the frequency of TSTG behavior.

There had undoubtedly been other TSTG in my hometown of 50,000 who were transgendered; using the 1% TG and .1% TS estimates, my hometown would have had an expected number of 500 MTF with 5 being transsexual but I had no way to make contact with them. At college the expected number of TG would have been about 35 MTF with about 3-4 being transsexual. For a long time, the only transsexual that I was able to find from all classes of my college alma mater was a published TS author who was out and easy to find. However, recently I found another on Facebook. I know there are undoubtedly more out there, even though it was a macho all-male school.

I did not believe the Abnormal Psychology information indicating that what I had was a rare behavior disorder. But I did not know exactly what to believe. I thought that the only thing I could do was to keep my secret and keep on posing as a man for the rest of my life. When I thought about my TSTG, which I tried not to do, I was lonely and depressed but I put on a good face, appearing to be a happy person dealing with what came along. I stopped looking for others with TSTG and, in fact, did not meet a second TSTG for almost 25 years. Or so I thought. The reality was that they were all around me and I had no way of identifying them.

My Abnormal Psychology course did not help me understand the biopsychology of TSTG because the teacher concentrated on how to give diagnostic tests including the Rorschach inkblot and the textbook did not have descriptions of various categories. Every once in a while, the teacher would let some information slip that he probably was not supposed to do according to the curriculum. At the time, the word gender was not even used because people believed that what we now call gender behavior was inextricably linked to sex.

The terminology associated with TSTG was confusing then and continues to be confusing. I only recently reached some consistent definitions, just to keep things straight in my own mind.

❖

We can now start to define some terms related to TSTG from a scientific, behavioral point of view. Warnings! Some of these definitions run against current public usage! Even if you think you know all these terms, you do not! Humpty Dumpty, notwithstanding, for the purposes of my research I had to make up my own definitions to insure that the terms were objective, descriptive, non-pathological and consistent. You can use them or not as you see fit but I want to be clear with my thoughts.

First of all, I distinguish *sex* being an assignment based on physical sex organ characteristics (e.g. male or female) usually at birth. Sometimes, more often than people believe, sex at birth can be ambiguous (more about this below). *Sexual behavior* includes those behaviors involving sexual arousal and sometimes consummation usually through orgasm (practitioners of Tantra try to avoid orgasm). A large number of bodily organs and functions are involved in sexual arousal beyond the genitalia and many are "multi-use." The brain and its functions are the most prominent of those multi-use organs, but there are many others. *Sexual behavior* generally involves the intent to reproduce but, in humans, there are a wide variety of sexual behaviors that do not involve this intent. To some extent, gender behavior and sexual behavior interact because some gender behaviors are clearly aimed at generating sexual arousal in the observer, while many do not.

Gender behavior is defined as a behavioral presentation that may conform or not to culturally defined *gender behavior categories such as masculine or feminine, and boy or girl, man or woman.* Gender categories are constructed by cultures with expected, required gender behaviors. Some cultures have had more genders than two and there are wide cultural and historical differences in how gender categories are defined in terms of dress, comportment, verbalization and other behavior. Some Native American tribes had 3 and 4 genders and the 50,000 Hijra in India are defined as a third category. Some Native Americans recognize a person as being "two-spirit", meaning that the person has both genders. It is said that the "two-spirits" were often functioned as shaman, medicine men or artisans because of their understanding of people. They were able to practice skills of both genders. Some two-spirits would weave cloth one day and do battle the next, changing clothing from feminine to masculine.

In recent years, *gender has become a more polite word for sex,* which is scientifically imprecise and confusing. The terms sex and gender need to be maintained as distinct from one another. The irony is that this dual-use was originated by social scientists that wanted to be polite but should have been the first to understand their mistake.

I will not use gender as a synonym for sex because as Humpty Dumpty in *Alice and Wonderland* said in the opening quote of this chapter, I would have to pay it overtime. When I use the word gender I am referring to behavior; when I use the word sex, I am referring to bodily organs.

I am reminded of the absurdity of dual use of gender whenever I have to fill out at a form question like this:

Question 1: Please provide your gender.

___ Male

___ Female

I have no idea how to fill out such a form. Male and female do not apply to gender and, being in TS transition I am part way between male and female. The analogous question is also absurd:

Question 1: Please provide your sex.

___ Man

___ Woman

Man and woman do not apply to sex and since I have not gone full time with my dressing I am part way between man and woman presentation. The NIH has announced that it is generating model questions for use in health data categorization to deal with GLBT issues which, if adopted more widely, may remedy this situation.

In order to bring their sex organs into alignment with their gender predisposition, transsexuals will go through a period called *transition*. Many will have guidance from health care professionals and follow the guidelines of the World Professional Association for Transgender Health, formerly known as the Harry Benjamin Society but some will not. Transition usually begins with *hormone therapy* (HT), which is frequently miss-termed hormone replacement therapy. The term hormone replacement therapy does apply to hormonal treatment for post-menopausal females or older males. It applies to those who cannot produce sufficient natural hormones. But a MTF TS takes drugs to increase normally low estrogen and progesterone levels and a FTM TS takes testosterone to augment their normally low testosterone levels. MTF generally take estrogen, progesterone and one or more testosterone blockers (e.g. spironolactone, finisteride aka propecia). Hormone replacement therapy is a misnomer for TSTG treatment because there is no "replacement" of lost natural hormones involved.

At some point in transition, MTF TS may get *breast implants* if HT does not provide sufficient growth; this occurs about half the time. FTM may have *"top surgery"* to reduce the size of their breasts. Many MTF may have "facial feminization surgery" (FFS) or other cosmetic surgery to make them look more feminine.

TS may then move on to the *real life experience* (RLE), formerly called the real life test, changed to reflect the intent that the experience is not a pass-fail test. The purpose of the RLE is to insure that a TS is ready for full time living in a new gender category. Many TS do not go further in transition but some proceed to *genital plastic surgery* after a year of RLE.

Genital plastic surgery (GPS) is also a term under constant dispute. It has been inappropriately named variously as gender reassignment surgery, genital reconstruction surgery, gender confirmation surgery, sex reassignment surgery, and sex reconstruction surgery. GPS pertains to the culmination of TS transition in which plastic surgery is conducted on the genitalia to bring them into alignment with the gender predisposition of the TS. The other terms are total misnomers. These misnomer terms do not apply because TS already possesses a gender predisposition that cannot be changed or reassigned. Their gender does not require confirmation through surgery. You cannot reconstruct what you never had. This mix-up is, in part, a consequence of the dual use of gender for both gender and sex. GPS is more descriptive and consistent with the various types of genital plastic surgery done for other purposes. Although GPS for TS is commonly referred to as a sex change operation, we are currently not medically capable of changing all sex indicators and structures, although some day we will be able to change most of them. Attempts have been made at transplantation of female internal genital structures to allow for reproduction by women and someday MTF. Genetic therapy is on the horizon. Non-TSTG of both male and female sexes, as well as those with ambiguous sex organs sometimes undergo GPS.

Although assigned sex is the binary male/female in most cultures based on genitalia in about % 2 of live births, there is some ambiguity for those who have *differences in sexual development* (DSD), sometimes called intersex. It is best to ask first which term is preferred for a given person and culture, DSD or intersex. The old term "disorders of sexual development" is perceived as a pejorative and should not be used.

DSD can range from those with a simple undescended testicle to the *guavedoche* in the Dominican Republic and similar populations in Middle East. Undescended testicles are very common, affecting about 30% of premature births and 4% of male children born at term.

The guavedoche are born with sex organs that spontaneously change at puberty due to a genetic deficiency of an enzyme called 5-alpha-reductase which speeds up the conversion of testosterone to other hormones. This deficiency delays androgens from forming the genitalia until puberty. The Pulitzer Prize winning book "Middlesex" is based on the experiences of a person who changed from female to male in puberty because of this deficiency. Cultures have special categories for such individuals because they have accommodated them in their cultural norms and know that the change will be coming to special children. After puberty the *guavedoche* is capable of fertilizing a female.

The English words associated with differences in gender behavior categories are *masculine/ feminine, boys/girls, and men/women.* These do not necessarily correlate with sex or sexual orientation. The assignment to masculine or feminine behavior category is culturally determined and varies from culture to culture and time period to time period. At birth, one is usually assigned a certain sex based on external physical organs and assigned to a particular gender category based on the sex assignment. Males are expected to have a masculine/man/boy gender; females are expected to have a feminine/woman/girl gender according to the common cultural rules.

Cultural categorization of gender presentation can turn on the slightest detail. One does not call a Scotsman feminine if he is wearing a kilt with a sporran (belt purse) but if he is without his sporran, he is ridiculed for being feminine. Taking away a male's sporran is a form of petticoating or forcing someone to present in their non-assigned gender. Outside of the Scottish culture not many people would even notice.

Gender behavior may not be consistent with a culturally assigned gender category. There are many males with some feminine gender behaviors and many females with some masculine gender behaviors. Currently metrosexual male exhibits some feminine gender behaviors including getting manicures, dying and frosting of hair and adopting feminine mannerisms. Homosexual males are sometimes stereotyped as exhibiting feminine behaviors but this is not true for all gay males. For example, there are homosexual men, usually body builders and/or bikers, affectionately called "bears" who are clearly hypermasculine and not feminine at all.

The exact stimuli that trigger sexual arousal, discussed in the preceding chapter, seem to be independent of both sex and gender behavior category. Vinyl or leather clothing can turn a person on whether one is a male or female or whether one is masculine or feminine. As we have seen, sexual arousal depends on the initial presence of sensitivity, novelty and on learning.

Sexual orientation is independent from sex, gender behavior and sexual arousal and pertains to the sex one is attracted to for romantic love. The words here are attraction to male and female and bisexuality. *Gay* is usually reserved for same-sex oriented males but is gradually being used for lesbians as well. *Lesbian* refers to same sex attraction of females. *Bisexuality*, of course refers to being attracted to both sexes. There are also those who are *asexual* and not attracted by sex at all.

One last term that you should know for politeness sake is the term "transvestite" which has been replaced by the more neutral, behavioral term "crossdressing." *Crossdressing* refers to any kind of dressing and presentation of a gender to which a person was not assigned at birth and not just TSTG. For example, drag queens and kings also crossdress but for entertainment purposes, although some also engage in TSTG behavior off the stage.

Let us exercise the terminology a bit to prove its usefulness. A "bear" is a male, gay, masculine person who may get sexually aroused by leather. A "dyke" is a female, lesbian, masculine person who may get sexually aroused by leather. A "lipstick lesbian" is female, lesbian, feminine who may also be sexually aroused by leather.

Then there is the fearsome acronym, GLBTQQDA. So far we have gay (G), lesbian (L), bisexual (B) and transgender (T), differences in sexual development and asexual (A). As was indicated earlier, sometimes intersex (I) is used in place of differences in sexual development (D). In no instance should someone who is intersex or has a difference in sexual development be termed someone with a "disorder of sexual development." The "Qs" are queer and questioning. Queer (Q) currently refers to those who are different but prefer not to be categorized in terms of sex, gender and sexual orientation. Questioning (Q) pertains to those who are actively trying to decide about their sex, gender and sexual orientation. Currently, the term *"tranny"* should only be used by TSTG, although it is in process of being reclaimed by TSTG for effect.

None of the diagnoses in Abnormal Psychology seemed to fit what I knew first-hand about my TSTG. I knew I was not homosexual and, in fact, abhorred males and masculine excessive behavior that was all around me. I knew, not from the abnormal psychology course but from a behaviorist-learning course that I did not have a neurosis. No one had taught me to be a TSTG. I did not believe that I was a fetishist because TSTG was not ruining my life like the fetishists described in my course and I was not in acute distress about it. Yes, I would get sexually aroused when wearing women's clothing or make up but more important activities could delay this for weeks. I felt that I engaged in crossdressing behavior because I wanted to be a female woman and that was as close as I could allow myself to be. And I knew I was not diseased.

We have made some progress since my college days. Indeed, TSTG is on the verge of being written out of the mental health diagnoses. The next iteration of the DSM (diagnostic statistical manual) of mental diseases is supposed to substitute gender dysphoria and move it out of the disorder category. The hope is that, like homosexuality was removed in 1974, TSTG will eventually entirely be removed. Some TSTG do need mental health counseling but that is because they are having trouble getting along with culture or trying to manage their lives. But so do lots of other people without TSTG. And there are plenty of diagnostic categories for billing the insurance companies for treatment that are not TSTG oriented. None of the mental health professionals that I have seen have ever used a DSM category for TSTG. I certainly was depressed by the loneliness and fear of exposure was the main contributor to my anxiety.

I did learn some information from Abnormal Psychology that gave me hope. The professor let slip some information that was not in the book or the library that indicated that TSTG had occurred in many times and cultures. None of the mental health theories and syndromes fit that model. He talked about some character called the Chevalier d' Eon who played a role as a European spy, and as Lady Beaumont went back and forth between man and woman, England and France. Then there were the "transvestites" (sic) in isolated Pacific islands. I was so struck by this that I did not get the details down in my notebook and the library did no provide any details (although I was afraid to ask the librarian for help). But it led me to conclude that I could not see how TSTG could exist in isolated cultures and times unless it was naturally-occurring, biological phenomena. All evidence I have seen since then has confirmed this conclusion.

Wanting to keep up with my peers, I did try to pursue a sex life. I joined a fraternity, went on road trips to womens' schools and had dates for the "big college" weekends. I learned some appropriate superficial masculine gender behaviors for dating and treating women superficially as party animals. The women were still sexually arousing me as they did in high school but dating was okay because I could control and limit the timing. Most of the women all had to go home to their respective colleges that were 3-5 hours away by car. When the date was over, it was really over and I could breathe a sign of relief and get back to studying.

Our fraternity was so party-oriented that we spurned the usually fraternity activities when they interfered with our serious drinking and partying. There was usually a keg or two every night. No pledge raids. There was a hell night but that was more psychological than physical harassment. Not knowing what to expect, my entire pledge class was totally drunk by the time that hell night started and several had to be physically helped through the process. Just like "Animal House" we always had a black soul band for parties as opposed to the psychedelic bands in other houses. To the surprise any new band members, we hardly ever danced but instead treated their performance as a floorshow. Some band members were surprised that we were looking at them rather than dancing with our dates.

Pornography at college and in the fraternity was ubiquitous and stimulating but again controllable in time. Occasionally I would find some pornography that referred to TSTG males that I studied intently but tried not to make my interest obvious. It was usually conflated with some BDSM theme. It did not arouse me but occasionally caused me to be fearful of what I might become. This started my confusion between TSTG and BDSM that I was eventually able to resolve.

My interactions with my fraternity brothers went pretty well, although I only made one or two close friends. I found that I could usually control the timing and mode of interaction. I could be alone when I wanted to be, and deal one-on-one with each brother, rather than in groups that I could not control. Since by then I was studying 9 hours a day as well as playing football and ROTC, I used the social time to recharge my batteries and had no time to think of loneliness. Proving that the kitchen committee chairmanship was no political graveyard I rose to become the fraternity treasurer. I guess I was thought trustworthy by my classmates because I now controlled the funds for both the fraternity and the ROTC detachment.

There were few opportunities to crossdress during college, as I was observable most of the time in the dorm and fraternity house, during college activities and at home. So, since it was frequently very cold and I was bundled up in a parka and hood, I took to wearing lipstick when I was out walking around. Most of the time, no one noticed and I felt like I was expressing my TSTG self. Whenever it got too dangerous or as I entered my fraternity house, I could easily wipe off the lipstick with a tissue. When disposal of the tissue became a problem, I would just litter the campus. Sometimes when the snow melted, I could see the residue of the tissues in front of the fraternity.

❖

By going to an all-male college, I had obtained control of sexual arousal from women and control of interactions with men but I never got used to the loneliness. It kept coming back whenever I had time to think. The sexual arousal was somewhat contained but I no longer had girls to talk to. Girls had been my only close friends. I was lonely because of inauthenticity and missing out of meaningful relationships with women. At some point, the loneliness because too much to bear and I decided to have a steady girlfriend who became a future wife.

I did not believe anything that Abnormal Psychology had to say about TSTG except for the clues about TSTG being natural and ubiquitous, so I was less concerned about being labeled a "transvestite." But I had to keep my TSTG as secret.

I had done so well in ROTC that the US Army offered me a career appointment, similar to that granted at West Point and I was seriously considering accepting it. The attraction was that a military career might be exciting and because I did not know what I wanted to do next. Since I had been assigned to the Adjutant General Corps as a psychologist, I figured I would be protected from combat. AGC psychologists administered IQ and other tests and conducted human resources activities.

Because I had not responded immediately, my ROTC advisor called me in for counseling. He was a major who wore the patch of the Pathfinder. Pathfinders are the paratroopers that parachute into enemy territory in the dead of night in order to mark out landing zones for other paratroopers. He was clearly a courageous, committed military man. He confirmed that I had applied at graduate schools and then said "Cadet, if you accept this career appointment you immediately will be reassigned as an Infantry Branch officer. You will be in Vietnam in 4 months and dead in 6. No one from this school has ever been denied a deferment to go to graduate school. I strongly recommend that you apply for a deferment and save your own life." So much for his approval of the Vietnam War. Coming from an established military man, this had a lot of weight, so off to graduate school I went with a commission as a reserve second lieutenant intending to work off my 2-year military commitment when I finished.

Chapter 3 References

Brown, G. (1988) Transsexuals in the military: flight into hypermasculinity. Archives of Sexual Behavior. Vol. 17, No. 6, 1988.

Conway, L. (2001-2002) How Frequently Does Transsexualism Occur?, 2013. http://ai.eecs.umich.edu/people/conway/TS/TSprevalence.html

Olyslager, F. & Conway, L. (2007). On the Calculation of the Prevalence of Transsexualism. *WPATH 20th International Symposium*. Chicago, Illinois, September 5-8.

Reed, B., Rhodes, S., Schofeld, P., & Wylie, K. (2009). Gender Variance in the UK. GIRES, June.

CHAPTER FOUR

Neuroanatomy and Graduate School

Are you some kind of a scientist?
Sir, I am every kind of scientist.
-Dr. Who

In 2000, I was stunned by the headlines that researchers from the Netherlands had discovered a "gender center" in the hypothalamus of the brain. This study found that the size and cell count of this "center" in MTF TS was more similar to females than to males. Since then, this finding has often been cited by biopsychology textbooks and other publications as an explanation of TSTG. Unfortunately, it also has been used as proof of a biological cause for TSTG in order to legitimize TSTG as meriting civil rights. This is totally unnecessary. The history and cultural spread of TSTG is enough to show that it is biological and part of natural diversity. And everyone should have the civil rights they deserve, no matter who they are.

I immediately doubted the conclusion of this study because of my graduate experience concerning the biopsychology of the hypothalamus. This chapter will describe the evidence for why I believe the conclusions of this study and the headlines are incorrect. It will also cover my graduate school experience.

———————— ❖ ————————

Graduate school gave me back the opportunity to crossdress and the intellectual freedom to learn about all of the sciences involved with neuroscience or biopsychology. I also thought if I got married that I could dispense with crossdressing but like so many other TSTG before me, I was wrong about marriage "curing" me.

I got married in part because I hoped that I would no longer be lonely and because I wanted a normal life. But the loneliness persisted through the courtship into marriage and beyond. I was not even sure that I understood TSTG and I that there was no way she would understand it.

Because I was now married and in graduate student housing, I had many uninterrupted opportunities to crossdress. My wife worked far enough away that walking was out of the question and she had no place to park, so I had the car. I would go home in the afternoons after class and work on statistical analysis of the data from my experiments. I would then don pieces of feminine clothing. I had bits and pieces of my mother's clothes that I had stolen from her and could wear some of my wife's clothing. I augmented these with lingerie from the local thrift store. I kept my female clothing in the back room where out-of-season clothing was kept. If my wife suspected my crossdressing or found these items, she never let on.

Now that I could crossdress *ad libitum*, I noticed several behavioral phenomena. After all, I was learning to be a psychologist and observe behavior, so I began to observe my own. There were three phenomena that I detected. The first was, of course, that the clothing initially aroused me. After a while the arousal subsided but I continued to wear the clothes because they felt feminine. I would become bored with just the experience of focusing on feminine clothing and turned on the TV or do some work. This was the time when Bobby Fisher and Boris Spassky were playing their chess "match of the century" and the TV was just able to pick up the play by play on a far away channel. I was interested in the match because of the Cold War implications and because I had never played chess very much and wanted to learn. There I was, watching chess and doing statistical analysis while dressed in feminine clothing. I keep adding to my clothes collection that became a problem because I had limited storage space. I found an access door to the attic crawl space and this provided some extra capacity.

The second phenomenon was that I would periodically feel guilty about crossdressing and would have intense fear of being discovered. That was when the "purges" hit. I would take all of the clothing that I had accumulated, put it in a garbage bag and discard it in some discrete location like a dumpster far from the university. I would then feel safe for a couple of weeks until I acquired a new piece of female clothing and accumulate clothing until the next purge. I purged every 4 months or so and the cycle would repeat itself.

The third phenomena I noticed was that if I was unable to crossdress for more than a couple of weeks, I became more and more agitated. Two weeks of vacation were manageable but if the time period got to be more than six weeks, I became desperate to crossdress.

The lipstick game that I had started in college continued. It was now made more interesting because, since this was the 60s and nearly anything was allowed. I had a curly mop top and wore bell-bottoms. I could wear lipstick while walking around the town even in good weather, not just when I was bundled up for winter.

I reported to the Psychology Department for graduate education. I tried to find friends in the psychology department and was successful in finding a somewhat mysterious lecturer with whom I could talk freely about psychology and who would eventually become a mentor and friend. He was near the end of his career and writing a book. The psychology department seemed to carry on their business but they were clearly distracted by Vietnam War protests. Faculty members would disappear for several days at a time to conduct anti-war activities. Teaching and research were interrupted by student strikes and demonstrations against the war. And most personal to me, the local ROTC detachment building was fire bombed with a Molotov cocktail. Since I was an officer in the US Army, I withdrew even more; fearing that somehow I would be targeted, or worse, that I would be called up to go to Vietnam. I did my best to fit into the counterculture, with long curly hair, jeans, peace jewelry galore and only an occasional bath. My biggest fear came when, once a year, I was required to get the department chairman to sign a US Army form saying that I was making satisfactory progress towards a Ph.D. degree. He was a top-flight psychologist but just about everyone in the department was against the Vietnam War. I did not know how he felt about my being in the US military. I was afraid to ask.

My only respite from research and loneliness was hanging out with the mysterious lecturer who kept late hours. He was an interesting character who had turned down his Ph.D. because he felt that his thesis did not constitute a "major advance in the field", even though it took up 4 long publications in a major psychology journal. He did receive a master's degree but the university had mistakenly awarded him a diploma in "Forestry" rather than Psychology. He always joked that he had another career to fall back on; he could always become a forest ranger. He was an intellectual in exile but the department provided him with office space and he gave an occasional lecture, usually on the history of psychology. He personally knew all of the famous psychologists and the animal behaviorists and as many of them delivered talks in the department, it was obvious that he was not just name-dropping. He was my link to classic psychology and together we drank late into the night, played tennis during the day and talked psychology incessantly. I reviewed his book drafts and he provided support to me to deal with the anti-war distracted faculty and reduced my loneliness.

I was attracted to biopsychology (physiological psychology or neuroscience) because it is an attempt to understand the basis of behavior without any boundaries. Before biopsychology, psychologists conducted hit-and-run investigations into other sciences such as neuroanatomy. But biopsychology embraces all of the potential kinds of sciences that might affect behavior. It encompasses the structure of the nervous system (neuroanatomy), the effects of various chemicals on the brain (neuroendocrinology, neuropharmacology), the functions identifiable in the brain and nervous system (neurophysiology), the behavioral of DNA genetics and non-DNA epigenetics and many other sciences. It involved electronics, chemistry and mathematics and biology. It was with this orientation that I worked on mastering the scientific knowledge affecting behavior. As Dr. Who says in the quote that begins this chapter, I would become "every kind of scientist." The common thread was to understand how behavior occurred.

My first love became neuroanatomy. I could see that the structures in the brain and nervous system had been painstakingly studied over many years before me. I could see neuroanatomists bent over their microscopes all night long, looking at and describing the structures that they saw. The beauty of neuroanatomy was seductive. The other reason that I love neuroanatomy is that whatever we determine in the other biopsychology sciences it will have to be related to places in the brain and nervous system because they are not homogenized, logical structures.

The brain and nervous system function as massively parallel analog computers, not the digital computers that humans build. The structures and functions in them are mechanisms that have survived over 500 million years of evolution. Some of them are very small, like the little mechanism at the base of the brain that keeps time with a DNA clock and influences diurnal rhythms. Some mechanisms, like motor control systems are comparatively massive and take up relatively huge volumes in the brain and nervous system. The spinal cord cannot be omitted because the basic information needed to walk or run or perform other complex behaviors is contained in the spinal cord. Also included in the spinal cord and related structures are the nervous system mechanisms that control the final path to sexual arousal, erections and orgasm. Many of the mechanisms are leftovers from previous species. Almost all of them operate unconsciously and are totally out-of-control from conscious thought. The brain and nervous system are magnificent and they do not easily lend themselves to simplistic labels or theories of operation that might be contrived by human beings. They just work. The mechanisms that work or at least do not interfere with reproduction are passed on to future generations.

The part of the brain and nervous system that was of most intense interest during my time in graduate school was the hypothalamus. If you put your tongue on the roof of your mouth, the hypothalamus is a few fractions of an inch above your tongue. During my graduate school time, many psychologists saw the hypothalamus as the critical part of the brain that caused behavior to occur. Based on a several particular findings in (Hetherington, A. & Ranson, S. 1942; Stellar, E. 1954) the hypothalamus was seen to contain centers for all basic behaviors. The 1942 finding just cited was that, if a particular part of the hypothalamus were destroyed (the ventromedial nucleus which is, as the Latin name suggests, is at the bottom-middle of the hypothalamus) rats would overeat and put on fat and weight to preposterous levels. The potential related finding was that destruction of areas lateral to the ventromedial nucleus caused rats to stop eating, lose weight and die without forced feeding. The third finding was that small electrical currents applied to lateral hypothalamic tissue would in rats produce, such behaviors as eating, drinking, sex, mouse killing and rat pup retrieval. The lateral hypothalamus contained a center for feeding and the ventromedial nucleus, next store, became the satiety center. The electrical currents in many hypothalamic locations also seemed intensely pleasurable and would induce rats to voluntary press a lever to near exhaustion to get more electrical stimulation. The feeding and other centers were linked to reinforcement and hedonistic theories of motivation.

These findings were the basis for the "center" theory of behavior. The notion was that there were centers for all behaviors in the hypothalamus. The centers were modulated by chemicals, the state of energy in the body, the state of water balance in the body or the need to mate. They somehow created these behaviors. The hypothalamus was responsible for regulation of internal states and their relationship to behavior.

I could literally walk through the laboratory and see very fat and very skinny rats, animals pressing levers to get a brain stimulation, animals forced to eat or drink by minute levels of electrical stimulation, male animals forced to have sex or kill mice whenever the electricity was turned on. All this was magic, but from the first I was skeptical, mostly because the center theory seemed too good to be true.

Even in my time at graduate school and the center theory began to unravel and been refuted. It did trigger a lot of valuable biopsychological research as it unwound, as theories often do.

For openers, the reward locations were ultimately linked to neurons containing dopamine; release of which we know is intensely pleasurable. For example, cocaine and amphetamine cause release of dopamine.

Rather than destroying a satiety center, destruction of areas near the ventromedial nucleus were linked to changes in metabolic rate, the burning of calories. This prevented the animals with ventromedial damage from losing weight. It was discovered that areas other than the ventromedial nucleus, also produced over-eating. The ventromedial nucleus itself was implicated in modulating estrous and menstrual cycles. The areas lateral to the ventromedial nucleus where destruction stopped eating and drinking were discovered to be motor pathways. With destruction of this area, animals literally could not execute the motor movements required for eating and drinking. With training, electrical stimulation could produce drinking instead of eating or eating instead of drinking, so there was no behavioral specificity for the "center" locations.

The *coupe de grace* for the specificity of electrical brain stimulation to produce behavior was the finding that tail pinch (placing an alligator clip, like a clothespin) on a rat's tail would also produce eating, sexual behavior and maternal behavior (Caggiula, 1972, Antelman, 1976; Caggiula, et al. 1976, Szechtman, 1977). In research circles, both electrical brain stimulation and tail pinch became known as "kick in the ass" phenomena.

The less flashy concept of what the hypothalamus does was available then and still is there now. The hypothalamus readies the body for behavior through the spinal cord, autonomic nervous system and the pituitary gland. For example, there are direct connections from/to the hypothalamus and the penis/clitoris that were found by a clever technique of infecting tissue with a safe virus in the hypothalamus or in the penis/clitoris and tracing the virus to the end of the chain of neural pathways. This is presumably how the hypothalamus influences sexual arousal in penile erection and female mating reflex behavior.

In 2000, I was surprised by the headlines that researchers from the Netherlands had discovered a "gender center" in the basal nucleus of the stria terminalis of the hypothalamus or BNST (Kruijver F., 2000) (I will explain about the BNST below). Due to my experience with hypothalamic "centers", I was immediately skeptical. Post-mortem comparison of male and female brains indicated that this particular hypothalamic nucleus, the basal nucleus of the stria terminalis (BNST) was larger in males than females (Zhou, 1995). MTF TS were more like females in size. So powerful is the appeal of "center theory" that this paper is often still cited in textbooks to prove that there is a natural biological structure in the brain for gender that causes TSTG.

The brain and nervous system are often characterized as something difficult to understand, mysterious and very complicated but the fundamentals are easy. The brain consists of cells like the rest of the body. The most important cell type to understand is the neuron that integrates information from neurons and communicates this information in turn to other neurons. Each neuron reaches out to other neurons by extending itself in structures called axons, sometimes over long distances. The longest neuron axon is one in your leg that is about 3 feet long. We tend to think of these axons as electrical transmission lines although the transmission more like a chemical disturbance that travels the length of the neuron axon. It is not a flow of electrons as in your house electrical system. Neuron cell bodies tend to cluster into structures in the brain and spinal cord called nuclei and they tend to group together to form nerves and bundles.

So it is with the BNST. It is a nucleus composed of cell bodies that form a bundle of axons called the stria terminalis (stria is Latin for string). The stria terminalis connects two very old anatomical structures in the brain. It connects the amygdala (the neuroanatomists had named it the almond in Latin because of its shape) that is a group of nuclei that integrate the interpretation of stimuli. The amygdala seems to be the place where the appropriate emotional response to current conditions is determined, for example, sexual arousal and fear and other emotions. This information is then sent to the hypothalamus for execution. The hypothalamus implements this emotional response through the descending autonomic nervous system to control heart rate, stomach motility, blood distribution to the skin and sexual reflexes. The hypothalamus also controls the mechanisms for secretion of appropriate hormones for stress, body temperature and other processes through the pituitary that is at the bottom of the hypothalamus.

Before animals evolved a cerebral cortex, the amygdala and hypothalamus and their connections were performing their functions very nicely. They are present in current species that do not have a cerebral cortex, like the birds and lizards of today. When the cortex began to grow in size during phylogeny or evolutionary development, it pushed the amygdala away from its original position. As the cortex grew it pushed the amygdala in a spiral "rams horn" path. The stria terminalis must have still been advantageous or at least not obstructive of reproduction because continued its connection between the amygdala and hypothalamus and thus now also follows this spiral course.

Analysis and scientific studies have revealed that the "gender center" BNST paper had some gaping flaws in its conclusions. The most obvious was that almost all of the MTF TS in the Netherlands study were under hormone treatment in transition from male to female at the time of their deaths. There was only one MTF TS who served as a "control group" who had ostensibly not been on hormones. Because she was dead, this could not be confirmed and TS are widely known to obtain hormones without their doctor's knowledge. Dispensing sex hormones without a prescription is not illegal in many parts of the world and birth control pills are easy to come by. Was it possible that illicit TS hormones could have changed the BNST to make it smaller in this one "control" MTF TS? The answers started to flow from research studies.

Since both the amygdala and hypothalamus have structures whose size varies with testosterone levels in animals, it was plausible that the effect observed in the Netherlands TS's was due to the reduction in the testosterone and testosterone blockade drugs that MTF TS take during hormone therapy in transition. A longitudinal MRI study of MTF TS showed that this was indeed true. Six months after starting TS hormonal therapy the base of the brain where the hypothalamus is located was radically changed. When compared with pre treatment MRI scans (Pol,

2006) the size of hypothalamic structures decreased. The brain actually shrunk an average of 30 cc in the hypothalamus area; this is equivalent to the size of the contents of two shot glasses! Such rapid shrinkage had never hitherto been observed except in trauma or disease. But the MRI did not have good enough resolution to assess the effects on individual structures such as BNST shrinkage or cellular changes. So follow-up studies are needed. And the study was only done for MTF TS. Could it be that the size of brain structures actually increases with testosterone FTM TS therapy? Such studies are currently underway.

If one considers additional evidence, it appears that various BNST related structures in the hypothalamus and amygdala are associated with sexual behavior and aggression in animals and that these are influenced by testosterone. They have direct connections to genitalia as previously indicated. But this system seems confined to sex and aggression (McCarthy, 2008) and is not a "gender system."

Since the BNST, stria terminalis and hypothalamus structures have been around since the lizard days of brain evolution, it stands to reason that gender is more complicated and more recent than these primitive amygdalo-hypothalamic structures that influence the reflexes underlying sexual behavior and aggression. It is more likely that gender predisposition is more like other psychological functions such as learning and memory and mediated by multiple brain and nervous system structures. Maybe the predisposition to gender is a newly evolved function and represented widely in the brain in humans, and maybe it is only made active through DNA and/or epigenetics. (Epigenetic factors include mechanisms that influence the brain, nervous system and body during development that modify DNA, alter DNA expression or are transmitted by parents separately from DNA.) In Chapters 7 and 8 we will see that this is not as far-fetched as it may seem.

There have been many other comparative neuroanatomical studies of male and female brains that have shown significant differences (Allen et al., 1990; Breedlove, 1990 Garcia-Falgueras, 1994). And there are incidental reports of TSTG having temporal lobe injuries or pituitary tumors. These studies usually cite the presumed extreme rarity of TSTG as evidence that these phenomena are responsible for TSTG. This notion was refuted in Chapter 1. So far, none of these anatomical differences has been shown to be convincingly associated with TSTG.

❖

I thought that marriage would cure me of TSTG. I thought that having a regular sex life and spousal companionship would address the loneliness and would reduce the need for cross-dressing. Like many other TSTG before me, I was wrong. As I said earlier in this chapter, the compelling need to express a different gender interfered with marital sex life, which was not fair to my spouse. I realized that the loneliness would not go away, no matter what I tried. I would be lonely anytime, anywhere, as soon as my wife or my work or something else did not distract my thoughts.

Fortunately, my TSTG had not been discovered by my spouse and as far as I know had not been discovered at the time I came out to her. The mode of discovery is important on the impacts for resolution of resulting relationship problems and in potentially staying together. My wife had not discovered my clothing stash or my small makeup collection at home, nor caught me in the act and would not do so during our marriage. When wives are surprised to discover their spouses TSTG by finding evidence, the emotional reactions are extreme when compared with revealing TSTG through serious conversation. Even then, there are emotional repercussions and loss of trust that are more complex and severe than any other marital problem. Unless they see discover their spouse crossdressed *en drag*, their first thoughts are usually that their spouse has been cheating on them and that the clothing or other evidence belongs to the rival.

If the spouse buys the story that that the evidence is due to TSTG, there is a very slow realization of the implications. In most cases, these implications cannot be fully anticipated by the TSTG, and can only be anticipated by one of the rare counselors experienced with TSTG phenomena. The initial thoughts of spouses are usually that they have been lied to by the TSTG and that is exactly right. Because invariably the TSTG has been expressing alternative gender behavior from an early age, the spouse may feel that the marriage was entered into fraudulently.

The next set of implications has to do with the spouse questioning their own sexual orientation. Were they inadvertently attracted to the TSTG because of their own same-sex desires? Does the fact of the marriage mean that they are really lesbian or gay?

If the offended spouse keeps the secret of TSTG, they are prone to suffer the same loneliness and situational depression as the TSTG themselves. If they do not keep the secret, they risk rejection. Keeping the secret, even if the marriage breaks up, is a toxic burden until it is no longer a secret. The offended spouse must constantly keep the secret in mind in order to keep from telling it which interferes with normal thinking and activities. The toxicity of secrets can spread to others.

Spouses are afraid that their families, friends, subculture and church will reject them if they share the TSTG secret. And they are exactly right. Cultural understanding of TSTG is increasing but still relatively rare and many social institutions hold dogmatic attitudes about TSTG. Spouses rightly fear that shunning will ensue if their TSTG comes out. They will drop in status and lose contact with those close to them.

Many spouses will believe that there must be a "cure" for TSTG, since we have such good medical science. But there is no present cure. Many TSTG and spouses may not know this fact and but still seek treatment for a cure, although some TSTG say that they would not take a cure even if one were available. It is no wonder that the charlatan business of "reparative therapy" still continues. Even among upstanding mental health professionals there is still general ignorance of TSTG but all reputable mental health professional organizations have declared "reparative therapy" to be useless and potentially injurious.

Even if all of these issues are addressed, the TSTG and spouse do not realize that, for many TSTG, the march from being transgendered to transitioning as a transsexual is inevitable. A common TSTG joke is "what is the difference between a TG and a TS?" and the common flip answer is "two years." Knowing that this often happens, spouses and certain support groups like Tri-ESS concentrate on regulating TG activities and preventing transition to TS.

If the marriage has produced or adopted children, there are significant issues with acceptance by the children of the marriage. It should be noted that most TSTG do manage to reproduce, so if there is a genetic or epigenetic component to TSTG it is passed on to the gene pool. Indeed, some pre-op FTM TS have actually birthed children after temporary cessation of their hormone regimen.

I survived the Vietnam War by going to graduate school and that made me feel a little guilty but it was what I really wanted to do anyway. When I had to go get my Army "making progress towards the degree" form signed for the last time by my department chairman and after he had signed it, I asked him how he felt about it. It amazed me that rather than getting a ration of anti-war rhetoric, he said, "anything that keeps people out of the war is fine with me." It never dawned on me that by signing my form he believed that he was pursuing the antiwar effort in a very practical way.

My friend, the lecturer finally published his book. It was provocative and revolutionized our thinking on the evolution of human behavior. He has become a revered psychologist by many. I am not one of these fans. Having a friend with whom I could talk psychology was plenty enough for me.

After receiving my Ph.D. from graduate school I planned to serve my 2-year active duty commitment in the Army, expecting to do psychology activities for military personnel needs. While my classmates were applying for jobs to various universities, I continued my research and began to pack up my things. (I also purged my feminine clothing.)

But the Army had other ideas. They reclassified me to the Medical Service Corps Branch and sent me to San Antonio for officer branch training for 90 days with no commitment for me to be on active duty beyond that. (Medical service corps officers spare doctors from administrative tasks, fly helicopters for medevac and some, the Allied Sciences, do medical research on Army topics.) The result was that I was out of a job with no prospects to get one, the academic job pursuit season being over.

I had to find a job quickly, so I asked around and got a list of all of the psychologists in the US Army which totaled about 35. I wrote to all of them, asking for a job.

It turned out that the skills and knowledge I had gained in studying the hypothalamus were of intense interest to the Army scientists involved in developing new antidotes for chemical weapons and agents. Many of these antidotes had effects on the hypothalamus and I had some of the surgical and experimental techniques to study them. A job with these scientists was ideal for me and came with guaranteed research funding and resources that I would have to scrabble for if I had gone to academia. As a TSTG, I was looking for a worthwhile problem to occupy my thoughts and give me a reason to go on and they had a problem to solve that was critical in the Cold War as well as save lives from civilian insecticide poisoning. It would be exciting to stay in the military where I could use both my knowledge of military science and biopsychology. But there were significant bureaucratic difficulties in reassigning me while I was still on active duty for training. Fortunately, the laboratory director for chemical defense was one of the most senior medical doctors in the Army at the time. One trip to Washington by him and I was on my way to a new job to fight the Cold War and conduct biopsychology research.

Chapter 4 References

Allen, L., & Gorski, R. (1990). Sexual orientation and the size of the anterior commissure in the human brain. Proceedings of the National Academy of Sciences. Vol. 89, 7199-7202, August 1992.

Antelman, S., Szechtman, H., Chin, P., and Fisher, A. (1975). Tail pinch induces eating sated rats which appears to depend on nigrostriatal dopamine. Science 189, 731-733.

Breedlove, S. (1994). Sexual differentiation of the human nervous system. Annual Review of Psychology 45, 389-418.

Caggiula, A. (1972). Shock elicited copulation and aggression in male rats. Journal of Comparative and Physiological Psychology. 80:393-407.

Caggiula, A., Shaw, D., & Antelman, S. (1976). Interactive effects of brain catecholamines and variations in sexual and non-sexual arousal on copulatory behavior of male rats. Brain Research. 111: 321-336.

Garcia-Falgueras A., & Swaab D., (2008). A sex difference in the hypothalamic uncinate nucleus: relationship to gender identity. Brain. 131, 3132-3146.

Hetherington, A. & Ranson, S. (1942). American Journal of Physiology. 136, 609-617.

Levay S., (1991). A difference in hypothalamic structure between heterosexual and homosexual men. Science. 253, 1034-1037.

Kruijver F., Zhou J., Pool C., Hofman M., Gooren L., & Swaab, D. (2000). Male-to-female transsexuals have female neuron numbers in a limbic nucleus. Journal of Clinical Endocrinology and Metabolism. 85(5), 2034-41.

Marson L., & Murphy A. (2006). Identification of neural circuits involved in female genital responses in the rat: a dual virus and anterograde tracing study. American Journal of Physiology. 291(2), R419-28.

McCarthy, M. (2008) Estradiol and the Developing Brain. Physiology Review 88, 91–134.

Pol H., Cohen-Kettenis P., Neeltje, T., Van Haren E, Peper J., & Brans R.G.H. (2006). Changing your sex changes your brain: influences of testosterone and estrogen on adult human brain structure. European Journal of Endocrinology. 155, S107–S114.

Rowland, N., & Antelman, S. (1976) Stress-induced hyperphagia and obesity in rats: A possible model for understanding human obesity. Science 191:310-312.

Stellar, E., De Gascun C., Kelly J., Salter N., and Lucey J. (1954). The Physiology of Motivation. Psychological Review. 5-11.

Szechtman, H., Siegel, H., Rosenblatt, J. & Komisaurk, B. (1977). Tail-pinch facilitates onset of maternal behavior in rats. Physiological Behavior. 19:807-809.

Véronneau-Longueville F., Rampin O., Freund-Mercier M.J., Tang Y., Calas A., & Marson L. (1999). Oxytocinergic innervation of autonomic nuclei controlling penile erection in the rat. Neuroscience. 93(4), 1437-47.

Zhou J., Horman M., Gooren L., & Swaab D. (1995) A sex difference in the human brain and its relation to transsexuality. Nature 378, 668.

CHAPTER FIVE

Pathology and the Cold War

"Show me a sane man and I will cure him for you."
-Carl Gustav Jung (1875-1961), founder of analytical psychology

For me, fighting the Cold War involved nearly continuous travel around the US. This allowed my crossdressing to get into full gear. For me, the Cold War was a two-front war. I had to develop technologies to defend against the Soviet Union on one hand but I also had to develop procedures to defend my crossdressing secret on the other.

For political reasons, the Cold War technology effort was fought across all of the US states. Each military system manager made sure that there were at least some components that were procured in each state and most Congressional districts. This insured funding for the system. As a human factors psychologist I traveled widely to assist the US government to select the right technologies and insure that humans could actually operated the systems under construction. I could go to another town where no one knew me, buy clothing and make up and dress in my hotel room. Most of the time I would stay in my room but occasionally I would go to a crossdressing support group where they had facilities at the meeting site to dress before the meeting. For the first time, I could completely present myself as a woman for short periods of time and meet other crossdressers.

At first I purchased my clothing at charity or distressed merchandise stores. I was a regular at the Salvation Army, Big Lots and wholesale stores. The clothing was cheap enough to discard in charitable donation bins, dumpsters or recycling centers. Cosmetics were easy to buy at local drug stores. Standard operational procedure was to order a pizza and buy a 6-pack before going to my hotel room. I would get dressed and made up and just sit watching television in my hotel room until I got bored and then get undressed and scrubbed up, take a shower and fall asleep. Taking a shower was critical to remove all traces of perfume from the cosmetics.

But I was soon dissatisfied with cheap clothing and bought dresses and skirt suits. This meant that I had to keep a stash of equipment at home and bring an extra bag on travel because I was dressing for two. I kept an extra suitcase and had to keep moving it around from basement to car trunk to office to evade detection. I usually checked the bag on flights and made sure it had my office address on the identification tag in case it got lost and had to be delivered back to me. This actually happened twice. When I did not check the bag, I worried about x-ray detection but no one ever challenged the bag contents. I even had to check the bag at the front desk of a military facility for a few hours. The outline of high heels was clearly visible in the outline of the soft bag but female clothing was no threat to the facility, so no one ever sensed anything worthy of alarm. I was always prepared to say that it belonged to my wife but no one ever asked.

In order to keep transcontinental travel costs down, I was always making connections somewhere in the Midwest. On the first return leg of each trip, I had time to think about my crossdressing and that created a danger zone for purging. The Midwest stopovers were littered with purged clothing, makeup and jewelry. Sometimes I would just abandon a bag at the baggage claim in the airport, hoping that someone or some charity would get some good from its contents rather than throwing its contents in the trash. Of course, in this day and age an abandoned bag would cause all kinds of airport security problems.

I was getting better information on TSTG at this point. Libraries now had books on TSTG. I read Jan Morris's Conundrum (Morris, 1974), a TS autobiography, and some books by Vern Bullough (one was Bullough, V., & Bullough, B., current edition 1993). Violating one of the prime directives to library patrons, I never took the books out of the library but instead hid them in the stacks until I had finished them. That way no one would know that I had read the books because they never were checked out. (If you were a library patron at the time, please forgive me for taking books illegally out of circulation.) While I generally trusted librarians, the digital record of who checked out what books could be read by library volunteers and others. In this digital age, know that privacy is even harder to maintain. You should know that today under the Patriot Act, the FBI has a legal right to see your library records by just asking. Facebook and Google customarily provide you email and information to the FBI and other law enforcement agencies if asked. If you are TSTG and in the closet, leave no trail behind.

I can vividly remember the opening scene of Conundrum with Jan Morris as a small boy under a piano. I began to believe that TSTG people were human after all and that authenticity was possible. The library also gave me access to fashion magazines that I studied in great detail.

The next channel for information was post office box rental. I got some useful information from a co-worker who rented a box to receive letters in response to her personal ISO (in search of) advertisements for dates. She told me that most of the time, they never asked for identification, but they probably do now. The mailbox allowed me to get books and magazines from the International Foundation for Gender Education including the magazine Tapestry and books by Virginia Prince. I particularly studied Virginia Prince "How to Dress Like a Woman, Though Male" (Prince, 1979), information I use to this day. In my situation, having limited storage space, buying a basic black skirt/pant suit that I could accessorize seemed the best alternative. Buying suit separates would allow me to get a bigger size top to accommodate my male shoulders and my smaller bottom. I became a compulsive Jones New York and Maggie McNaughton buyer for their conservative suits. That is, until Maggie McNaughton disappeared as a brand in the last few years. I lost my original copy of this book in a purge but recently found a copy to assist in writing this book.

The third source of new information was through computer bulletin boards. For those of you who were not active computer geeks in that era, a computer bulletin board was a private computer system that allowed you to dial-in over phone lines and access databases, chat and send emails long before the Internet became commonly available. Private bulletin boards were eventually replaced by for-fee systems such as CompuServe and AOL and I used them too. I could see pictures of TSTG, although I was careful not to provide one of myself. I was not as alone anymore. For the first time, I could reach out to other TSTG in near-real time. The communities that grew up through bulletin boards were continuous with today's Facebook, MySpace TSTG communities. The current unwritten rule is that all TSTG who are recognizable as TSTG are accepted as friends. This is against the websites rules of course. At one time I had 4500 Facebook friends on my page until Facebook pulled the plug. They demanded a photo id in my feminine name, which I did not have then, so I immediately lost connectivity with TSTG around the world.

Finally, my feminine clothing got too voluminous for one suitcase and for playing hide and go-seek. I was forced to rent a storage unit. I received my bill at work and paid in cash, so it was not traceable. And I got one of those erectable clothing closets so I could hang things and protect them from the inevitable dust of the storage facility. This was after I came out to my first wife and I got a storage unit with her encouragement in order that my kids would not find out my secret.

Even though I had left the Army and become a civilian contractor, the Cold War was a great distraction from my TSTG. The stakes were high and technology work was cutting-edge. There were real missiles and weapons pointed towards my children and me. Since I was working as a human factors psychologist, I got to learn about all sorts of intriguing job functions: photo interpreters, intelligence analysts, combat pilots, military police, ship pilots and aircraft weapon system operators. I got to go to places that hardly anyone knew existed and got to put my hand in the cold engines of both an SR-71 and U-2, the day before their missions. I learned enough about camouflage to become a talented camoufleur. I "bar-hopped" around Christmas parties that groups of intelligence analysts gave at work. Because of the alcoholic haze, I cannot remember the specializations of all of the groups I visited. They all were having a good time and, as in other organizations, vied to see who could have the best party. As for most warriors, I remember the good times but I suppress the bad ones.

I was unable to go see a mental health professional about TSTG because there was a ban on mental health counseling at my company. The ban was finally lifted because they had found that the ban did more harm than good and lifted it for marital counseling. This was not totally out of the goodness of their hearts, the employee still had to sign a waiver to allow the investigator to talk to the therapist and therefore they get a professional opinion on the employee's stability.

When I found out that they were now allowing mental health therapy for marital counseling, I immediately started talking to a therapist with the aim of getting help with my TSTG issues. This was not an artifice. I actually was having marital issues because of TSTG. My first psychologist was not specialized in TSTG issues but did do a lot of counseling for gays and lesbians. She was willing to learn about TSTG and knew about patient management resources, like who do you go to in order to help you get a feminine hair cut with no questions asked. However, she did no use a pathological description for TSTG on the insurance reimbursement.

I started investigating the pathological causes of TSTG that derive from the medical model. Mental health professionals, like other health professionals are taught the medical model. This model says that the health professional has to understand the cause of a pathological disease before he/she can diagnose and treat it. This requires the identification of a potential pathology. Since the mental health professionals were historically the first health professionals to be forced to deal with TSTG, it was logical to start there. I have to admit that part of my motivation for investigating these causes was to debunk them, just as I had learned in college and graduate school. But, as a scientist, I tried to keep an open mind. My sense was and still is that TSTG is not pathological in nature. But, of course, older mental health models in the Freudian era concentrated on such explanations.

I encountered the Diagnostic and Statistical Manual, otherwise known as the DSM that lists all of the mental health diagnoses, originally for standardization but later for insurance reimbursement purposes. The DSM is revised from time to time. My first encounter was with the second DSM revision aka "DSM II." (The latest DSM is DSM IV.) Over the years, I could saw that TSTG continued to be classified as pathological but I also witnessed a gradual depathologization of homosexuality and BDSM. Although the depathologization of TSTG lagged these other phenomena, it will purportedly start with DSM V that will be released later this year.

Most TSTG come to mental health professionals because they are having trouble dealing with family or culture, so there is really no reason to use DSM mental disorder categories. There are plenty of other billing categories that can be used to insure that TSTG get the help they need.

❖

Now that information sources were more readily available, I was able to make some progress in getting access to scientific studies of TSTG. I discovered over 60 suggested causes of TSTG, about half of which can be classified as pathological. Even if I thought that a suggested cause had no merit, I endeavored to look for any scientific evidence supporting it. I could access the National Institute of Medicine database and later PUBMED and had better access to library books. I figured I could also defend my research by saying I was a psychologist and most everyone assumes that psychologists have the license to study dark, weird phenomena anyway.

I have found that there are over 30 suggested pathological causes of TSTG that can be categorized into:
- Psychodynamic
- Organic disorders and
- Paraphilias.

PSYCHODYNAMIC
Psychodynamic causes postulate theoretical intervening variables or constructs such as mental states and interactions that are then used to ex-

plain the cause. These intervening variables and constructs are therefore inaccessible to direct observation or measurement unless the author can identify objective manifestations of these theories that can be observed and measured. This is referred to as operationalizing a theory. To me, any scientific cause of TSTG must pass this *prima facia* test.

A group of suggested psychodynamic causes comes from Freudian theory but none of these can be reduced to objective measurement or scientific study. These include:

- Neurosis
- Castration Anxiety and Pre-emptive Strike
- Transitional Objects due to same sex parent
- Rejection of one's sex including penile disgust
- Gender Envy
- Dissociation Personality Disorder

Neurosis is probably the best-known Freudian era pathological medical model. Inspired by the steam engines of the day, it involved postulation of elaborate mental forces resulting from childhood psychological injury that lead to inappropriate behavior. None of these hypothesized forces are accessible to observation and measurement and Freud was vague on how to operationalize them. The best we might do is to say that a neurosis is an inappropriate learned behavior due to some trauma but there is no evidence that TSTG behavior is a result of such a process.

The idea behind *castration anxiety* is that a MTF TSTG is so afraid that he will lose his penis that he preemptively has it cut off either figuratively (TG) and/or physically (TS). There is no way to objectively measure or test this theory. The literature does not even include an attempt to do so.

Charles Shultz drew on his experience and maybe his knowledge of Freudian psychology to give his Linus character a security blanket as a *"transitional object"*. As a potential cause of TSTG this theory indicates that one is still attached to the same-sex parent despite the Freudian notion that breaking this attachment is needed for proper psychosexual development. Thus under this theory, the feminine clothes that MTF TSTG wear and the masculine clothes that FTM wear become security blankets and eventually *"transitional" objects.* Again, there is no way to objectively measure or deal with this intervening variable. The literature does not even include an attempt to do so. Yet when I walked into a new psychiatrist's office several years ago for the first session he immediately diagnosed my crossdressing as an expression of a transitional object. I did not schedule a second session. Note that this use of transition is totally different from the transition that TS undergo to bring their bodies into better alignment with their gender predisposition.

While it is true that TS and some TG reject their sex organs and want them changed through surgery, *genital disgust* does not qualify as cause of TSTG. Genital disgust is an emotion and not an explanation. One would have to show why or how genital disgust originates. I can postulate some related potential causes but that may not be fair to the Freudians and, more importantly there is no evidence for them.

TSTG do envy people expressing gender behavior that they would like to be permitted to express themselves. For example, the MTF TSTG might be envious of an outfit that someone of the feminine gender is wearing. *Gender envy* does not qualify as an explanation for TSTG. I know I am envious of a woman dressed to the nines, not because I am attracted to her but for the art of her clothing and comportment style. Until I told her about my TSTG, my second wife did not understand that and assumed that I was being a typical ogling male. But again, envy is an emotion and not an explanation. One would have to show why or how gender envy originates and operationalize it. Again, I can postulate some related potential causes but there is no evidence for them.

Multiple personalities or *dissociative personality disorder* is a prominent non-Freudian pathological psychodynamic suggested cause of TSTG. However, the concept of multiple personalities or dissociative personality disorder is ill-defined and controversial phenomena even among clinicians. The idea is that people can have multiple personalities that are independent, cannot always be brought forward on demand and which may or may not have awareness of the other personalities. Most people have seen the movies, "The Three Faces of Eve" and "Sybil" which purport to provide example cases. It turns out that a lot of the phenomena describe in these movies was later found to be in error. Upon further investigation, the whole idea starts to unravel. The idea is that dissociative personality disorder is caused by early trauma, which we found in Chapter 1 does not appear to be true for TSTG. It is true that TSTG can change from gender role to gender role but there is no suggestion that these roles are separate from one another. Just as a person can play a role in a play, play a role in an athletic team and also play a role as a father, TSTG can play multiple roles but this is not the same as the concept of dissociative personality disorder. Of course, playing a role with which you are uncomfortable is exhausting, as many actors and TSTG have found.

At best, psychodynamic theories are a kind of "shorthand" or a reminder to clinicians about individual patients. Psychodynamic explanations rely heavily on intervening variables and concepts rather than observable behavior or empirical evidence. This makes it impossible to operationalize them or reduce them to testable scientific hypotheses. Many of them predict all possible behavioral outcomes. They may be theories, but they are not scientific theories.

At worst, psychodynamic explanations for TSTG are used by junk science commentators and sometimes the general public as pejoratives for TSTG behavior. They deliberately use pathology and psychodynamics to sell airtime, newsprint and now web content. Used in this way, these terms and theories are destructive to TSTG, and there is absolutely no science that backs them up.

Organic Disorders

Two potential organic causes of TSTG that have been advanced include depression and obsessive compulsive disorder.

TSTG are often treated for depression that results from conflicts between TSTG behavior and culture, making their depression a rational response to circumstances rather than an underlying organic physiological problem or illness. There evidence indicates that TSTG is not a result of depression (Coleman, 1990; Lam et al., 2004; Hepp, Kraemer, Schnyder,

Miller, Delsignore, 2005). The bottom line is that family and cultural-rejection situations in which TSTG find themselves can cause situational depression but organic depression does not cause TSTG.

The other organic disorder worth mentioning is obsessive-compulsive disorder (OCD) for which we now have extensive drug treatments. Although TSTG behavior might appear to be compulsive, most TSTG manage to function in society, delaying or deferring their need for preferred gender expression. Furthermore TSTG does not respond to drug treatments used for OCD.

Although there are a few reported isolated individual co-occurrences of TSTG with other organic disorders, such as schizophrenia, mental health professionals are expert in diagnosis of these organic disorders and they are not commonly associated with TSTG. Indeed, WPATH guidelines indicate that the clinician should rule out organic disorders prior to approving TSTG treatment or TS transition. The pathological term is "co-morbidity" which to most people sounds like something deadly. However, it really just means co-occurrence. Investigators often use the rationale that TSTG is so rare that the co-occurrence of TSTG with some other ailment must mean that the two are causally associated. As we saw in Chapter 1, the actual frequency of TSTG occurrence in the population is significant. One could argue, that it would be unusual *not* to find co-occurrences of TSTG with organic ailments.

PARAPHILIA

Paraphilia is a big, pejorative psychodynamic word that just means getting sexually aroused by unusual objects that interferes with normal behavior or causes distress. There are two types of suggested TSTG causes in this category: sexual fetish and autogynephilia.

People get sexually aroused by all manner of objects and stimuli. This does not become a paraphilia until it causes interference with normal activities to the point that an individual cannot function. Clothes associated with the other sex may arouse TSTG but that does not automatically cause interference with normal activities and the arousal tends to extinguish in TSTG. However, much of the public and many mental health professionals believe that TSTG engage in crossdressing because of the "cheap sexual thrills." This is probably because they get aroused themselves when they see or hear about crossdressing because it is a novel stimulus. Since, as described in Chapter 2, sexual arousal seems to obey the laws of classical conditioning, arousal in TSTG should be reduced or extinguished after repeated exposures and exposure time. Prince (1976) describes this extinction process and found that MTF TSTG continue to dress and exhibit opposite-sex gender behaviors, long after this extinction process has ended and the clothing and behaviors do not evoke sexual arousal anymore. My impression is that most TSTG also seem to be able to appropriately prioritize TSTG activities with other activities such as work, family and social relations so that there is no interference.

Another paraphilia-related theory, is autogynephilia, a term coined by Blanchard in 1989 and used by others (Lawrence, 2007; Ekins, and King, 2001) to describe MTF sexual "erotic arousal in association with the thought or image of themselves as women", or alternatively as "love of oneself as a woman" (Blanchard 2005) or alternatively as "love of women and want to become what they love" (Lawrence, 2007). Blanchard and Lawrence sometimes exclude arousal to feminine presentation and feminine behavior from this definition but instead substitute romantic arousal for sexual arousal.

As with other psychodynamic theories the problem with autogynephilia is that it cannot be operationalized sufficiently to conduct experimentation and test and therefore does not qualify as a scientific theory or hypothesis. The first sources of empirical proof offered by supporters involves questionnaire responses on a "core autogynephilia scale" (Blanchard, 1989) which only has face validity. This means that it only measures whatever it measures and no scientific evidence is available to underpin it. And the theory and scale contradict one another. There is plenty of psychological literature on questionnaire methodologies. It is known that it is impossible for subjects to respond to questions without visualization or recall of concept attributes (Bruner, Goodnow, Austin,

1967). In this case it is impossible for the TG to respond to the questions about the concept of themselves as a woman or the concept of love without visualizing or recalling what a woman looks like or how a woman behaves. For this reason, questionnaire items can never be made specific enough to exclude how the subject responds to clothing, feminine behavior, or romantic behavior from consideration. Since this exclusion is a tenet of autogynephilia theory, the existence of a scale has no meaning.

The only semi-empirical evidence cited to support autogynephilia is a physiological phaloplethysmograph study (Blanchard, & Ricansky 1986) in which MTF TG became sexual aroused as measured by penile blood pressure to stories of crossdressing. In this study, there was no attempt to actually operationalize a test for autogynephilia or isolate the concepts of the "idea of oneself as a woman" or the "love of oneself as a woman" from the structure of the crossdressing stories. Do the idea of oneself as a woman or love equate to sexual arousal? That is not stated in the theory but that is how it was operationalized in this experiment. If the theory of autogynephilia does equate to sexual arousal, then it devolves into the "cheap sexual thrills" fetish theory that we have already considered and discounted.

It is not surprising in the Blanchard/Ricansky study that the TG responded with sexual arousal to crossdressing stories. One would expect from classical conditioning extinction theory that the extinction (desensitization) of all of the conditioned stimulus-response connections between feminine clothing/behavior that took many years to establish (Chapter 2) should take multiple exposures and possibly several years. The Blanchard, Ricansky, Steiner study provided no empirical support to separate autogynephilia from "transvestic fetishism" through its design or results.

Since TSTG is known to be a naturally occurring, benign behavioral phenomenon--a conclusion supported by historical, cultural and biopsychology evidence (Decker & Pol, 1989; Witten, et al., 2003), it should not be considered an illness and should not be deliberately or inadvertently be pathologized by mental health professionals, by the public media or any other group. No doubt, TSTG occasionally need to seek mental health services for support and, for some, for treatment following WPATH guidelines. The guidelines are there to specifically rule out mental illness and mental incompetence in consideration of treatment or potential TS transition decisions.

———————— ❖ ————————

As the Cold War reached its peak, the need for new and improved aircraft sensors became more imperative. We had to have something the Soviets did not. I spent three years arranging flight tests of sensors on a grand and somewhat overwhelming scale. We would test many sensors at once on whatever aircraft in which they were currently installed, creating an "aluminum overcast" of aircraft. The aircraft were flown in a planned order, depending on their size and other factors. The included everything from helicopters, light aircraft, mid-level jets, large converted cargo airplanes and high-flying reconnaissance aircraft, some forty or so in all. The grand finale was always to fly the big jet aircraft at low altitudes that literally would scare local farm animals to death. On those days, we always had people out driving around with Ben Franklins to compensate farmers for their dead chickens and other farm animals. The big aircraft were always last because we knew that we would be soon asked to leave after their overflights. As a result of these tests and their analysis, I was asked to put a 5-year plan together for sensor development but then something happened that I did not expect—peace broke out.

Chapter 5 References

Blanchard, R. (1989). The concept of autogynephilia and the typology of male gender dysphoria. Journal of Nervous and Mental Disease. 177, 616–623.

Blanchard R., & Racansky I. (1986). Phallometric detection of fetishistic arousal in heterosexual male cross-dressers. Journal of Sex Research. 22(4) 452-46.

Blanchard, R., Zucker, K., Bradley, S., & Hume, C. (1995). Birth Order and Sibling Sex Ratio in Homosexual Male Adolescents and Probably Prehomosexual Feminine Boys. Developmental Psychology. Vol. 31 (1), 22-30.

Bullough, V. & Bullough, B. (1993). *Cross dressing, sex, and gender.* University of Pennsylvania Press.

Bruner, J., Goodnow, J., & Austin, G. (1967). *A study of thinking.* New York: Science Editions.

Coleman, E., & Cesnik J. (1990). Skoptic syndrome: the treatment of an obsessional gender dysphoria with lithium carbonate and psychotherapy. American Journal of Psychotherapy. 44 (2), 204-17.

Decker, R. & Pol, L. (1989). *The tradition of female transvestism in early modern Europe.* New York: St. Martin's Press.

Ekins, R., King, D. (2001). Transgendering, migrating and love of oneself as a woman. International Journal of Transgenderism. 5(3).

Hepp U., Kraemer B., Schnyder U., Miller N., & Delsignore A. (2005) Psychiatric comorbidity in gender identity disorder. Journal of Psychosomatic Research. 58: 259– 261.

Lam, H., Sunita A., Stewart M., Gabrel A., Leung M., Lee, H., Wong S. et al. (2004). Depressive Symptoms Among Hong Kong Adolescents:

Relation to Atypical Sexual Feelings and Behaviors, Gender Dissatisfaction, Pubertal Timing, and Family and Peer Relationships. Archives of Sexual Behavior. 33(5), 487 – 496.

Lawrence A. (2007). Becoming what we love: autogynephilic transsexualism conceptualized as an expression of romantic love. Perspectives in Biology and Medicine. 50(4), 506-20.

Mayer C., Kapfhammer H. (1995). Coincidence of transsexuality and psychosis Nervenarzt. 66(3), 225-30.

Morris, J. (1974) *Conundrum.* Harcourt Brace. (now 2006 NYRB Classics).

Prince, V. (1976). Understanding Cross-Dressing. Los Angeles: Chevalier Publications.

Prince, V. (1979). How to Be a Woman though Male. Chevalier Publications, Los Angeles.

Witten, T., Benestad, E., Berger, I., Ekins, R., Ettner, R., Harima, H., et al. (2003). Transgender and Transsexuality. Academia.edu. http://www.academia.edu/280714/Transgender_and_Transsexuality

Culture and Choice

*Because you didn't come here to make the choice, you've already
made it. You're here to try to understand <u>why</u> (emphasis added)
you made it. I thought you'd have figured that out by now.*
-The Oracle in Matrix Reloaded

The Berlin Wall fell and things started to change. As people began to
believe that the Cold War was over, there were small signs that they were
rearranging their lives. Initially, I did not have time to notice or think
about my future because I had committed to develop a program plan
for the next 5 years of the sensor development project. I worked on it for
three months straight and the last week before the deadline got about 4
hours of sleep in 2 days. The customer who had requested this plan had
moved on to another assignment so I delivered the plan to his replacement at 6 AM. He seemed totally uninterested. The delivery made, it
was off to the airport to return home.

The airplane was buttoned up and ready to go. We were still on the
tarmac ramp and waiting to taxi but we were delayed for a few minutes.
I tried to sleep but I was still wired from preparing the plan and deliver-
ing it. It was so cold, that I still had my trench coat and watch cap on.

It was then that I let myself realize that the Cold War was over. I no
longer had a purpose bigger than myself. I was not satisfied with my life
and I had to do something about it. Something was missing and since
the war was over, I was now willing to risk exposing myself by actually
meeting other TSTG and dealing with my secret.

I saw an article on TSTG support groups in, of all places, Time magazine. I started researching TSTG support groups but was disappointed
to find from their literature that they all met on weekends. I was not yet
ready to risk inquiries from my wife as to where I was during weekends.
I did however find out from my letters to the groups that there was an

advertisement for a BDSM group that had weeknight meetings and they were about to hold a meeting on crossdressing. To cover my tracks, I planned a trip a late night return and hopped an earlier flight that got me home late afternoon. To avoid discovery from a potential traffic accident I stashed my suitcase in my car in the airport parking lot and took public transportation.

The agenda for the BDSM meeting was just like any other hobby meeting that might be about knitting or woodworking but the dress was a little different. Most of the people were wearing leather or were wearing black. In turn, each person stood up and announced their name and interests. I used an assumed name and mumbled something about my interests based on the statements of previous talkers, not mentioning crossdressing. The meeting then turned to the night's presentation on crossdressing. It was clear that most of the people at the meeting were clearly involved with BDSM but there were several people who were recognizable TSTG. The presentation by the speaker concerned how to come out to your spouse if you were TSTG and was interesting but the discussion afterwards was even more interesting. Each of the TSTG present got up and talked. I can never forget the first TSTG that spoke. Cynthia was wearing a hounds tooth black and white skirt and white silk blouse. What was confusing was that Cynthia had a dominant mistress. The mistress proceeded to get up and described how Cynthia needed to crossdress and needed "training" from a mistress. To get complete transition from male to female required a mistress since being a women required skill and discipline. This overlap between TSTG and BDSM was a surprise to me. I certainly did not need or want a mistress to force me to crossdress.

I attended many meetings of this BDSM support group but they never took up the topic of crossdressing again and only occasionally would another TSTG appear. I did learn all about BDSM techniques, subculture and etiquette, which I found professionally but not personally interesting. After later separating from my first wife, I met a dominant woman in the group who took me to other BDSM meetings and parties. She was an expert in inflicting pain with the single-tailed whip but she was not interested in crossdressing. And although I found BDSM interesting, I was not into BDSM "scenes" or being whipped. We did have some common interest in writing and art. Our non-BDSM dates were at literary sites and art galleries. Although it would seem that BDSM people and TSTG have a lot in common, both engaging in taboo activities, I found that there was only a small overlap.

In my next exploration, I got the address for an out-of-town TSTG support group from a list of support groups in Tapestry (a magazine for TSTG, still being published by the International Foundation of Gender Education) and wrote to them, now that I had an anonymous post office box.

I told the point of contact from one group that although I was frequently in their city during weekdays, I could not attend weekend meetings. In reply, the person who was eventually going to become my guide and friend, suggested that I attend their couples group meetings that occurred on weekday nights. They were not advertised in the literature of the group. She told me to call her on the day of the next meeting and she would give me the location and time. I went to the next meeting and felt immediately welcome. I became a regular attendee, tailoring my travel schedule to be there whenever possible. There were usually several couples there but this was a heterogeneous group, some of the members were married, some were not. In some cases the wives knew about the crossdressing of their husband and attended, and in some cases the TSTG came alone because their wives did not know. Some were questioning and some just dropped in to say hello. One was a male model that went from boat conventions to car conventions to other trade shows. He was the handsome hunk you would see who decorated the merchandise. The model was questioning both his gender and his sexual orientation. Good thing he did not have to pose in shorts as a man because his legs were shaved up to mid-thigh.

Unlike other TSTG support groups, this was a pansexual group that accepted anyone without qualification as long as they behaved themselves.

There were people questioning their gender and sexual orientation in some cases simultaneously. I was surprised to learn that the crossdressers had diverse jobs that ranged from farmer, to post office mail deliverer to university professors, military, factory workers and, of course, male models. At the first meeting, my guide, Marjorie showed me a book by Mariette Pathe Allen full of beautiful pictures of TSTG. The book gave me hope that I could look feminine despite being male.

Although the pansexual group was my mainstay, I also eventually attended meetings in Los Angeles and Washington DC. The Los Angeles group meeting place and times were totally open and advertised in Tapestry. This group included androgynous males who weren't trying to follow any particular gender category norms but dressed and looked however they felt. This group seemed to have a disproportionate number of male nurses and some participants served as househusbands or housewives depending on how they categorized themselves.

Naturally, the group in Washington required more screening before entry. They set up a luncheon meeting to interview me and I passed without trouble. The location and time of the meeting was semi-secret and still is. The meeting was similar in format to other groups but the TSTG were different. It was no surprise that the group was composed of a cross-section of government and military workers in the Washington area. No farmers or factory workers. However, the biggest difference seemed to be that their skirts were very short, even for the older TSTG. At one of these meetings I met my first TS celebrity, Andrea James. This was long before she moved to California to build TS roadmap site and seek her fortune. She had a great presentation and was friendly towards me.

There is a scientific theory that maintains that support group culture is a factor in encouraging TSTG (Doctor, 1988). However, in the long term, TSTG do not usually stay with support groups. Support groups initially provide safe opportunities for TSTG to find themselves. They later find that support groups are not needed or only needed as a rally point before going to a nightclub. A few diehards do stay in the support group in order to help the newbies and journeymen TSTG. There are many more TSTG who never go to a support group meeting and find themselves through other experiences. The exception may be the Tri-Ess support groups whose main objective is to keep marriages together and contain TS emergence. Support groups do not seem to be a factor in long term maintenance of TSTG behavior because TSTG leave support groups when the TSTG no longer need them and many TSTG never go to support groups, anyway.

On the other side of the globe in India there is an interesting group of TSTG called the Hijra who have their own subculture that numbers over 200,000. Because of the repressive cultural environment in India against TSTG, the Hijra band together for both economic and social support. They have their own subculture because they are rejected by the larger culture of India. On the darker side, they perform their own non-medical castrations of TS. They are organized to provide entertainment at weddings, christenings or other affairs and, unfortunately, to beg. The Hijra really has no other way of making a living because they are banned from most jobs. This is changing slowly and the Hijra now have their own "third sex" marker on their identity cards and some are attempting to run for office. So the Hijra stay together, not because of some club or sororital organization but because they cannot enter into the Indian society at large.

Most of the time, culture is a negative causal factor in TSTG behavior because most cultures suppress and reject TSTG. Many are discouraged from expressing their preferred gender behavior and this can delay TSTG emergence. Culture often discourages gender and sexual exploration through censorship and social pressure.

TSTG are subject to the toxic results from keeping their TSTG condition secret and from related activities to express TSTG behavior. Secrets are toxic and interfere with authenticity. Authenticity is the concept of acting true to oneself. Inauthenticity interferes with creativity, relationships and happiness because one has to constantly calculate how to protect the secrets and this ties up too much brain processing capacity (Kelly, 1995).

My TSTG emergence was triggered by the fall of the Berlin Wall and the end of the Cold War. It is quite common for a significant life event to change behavior and not just TSTG behavior. Significant life events such as death of a spouse, change in a job, or a health crisis create what some call an "existential crisis" which must be resolved. TSTG often emerges or becomes more frequent after such life events. Some maintain that an existential crisis is one of the principal ways to change behavior and therapists sometimes try to provoke such a crises in patients to change their behavior (Yalom, 1980.)

There are four types of existential crises:
- Realization that you will die
- Realization that life has no intrinsic meaning
- Realization that we are forever isolated from one another
- Realization of free will

Significant life events can trigger one or more of these crises. For example, loss of a loved one obviously triggers the *knowledge of death crisis* but it may also trigger the isolation crisis because the dead person is gone. The ways in which existential crises are typically resolved is different for each type. For the death crisis, the resolution involves the determination to make the most of each moment remaining in ones life. In the case of TSTG who have suppressed their behavior from an early age, at some point the realization of future death means that they can no longer postpone TSTG expression.

The second existential crisis, the *loss of life meaning crisis,* is typically resolved by picking something to give life meaning. Part of my existential crisis was realizing that saving lives in the Cold War had given my life meaning that this was now over. I did not immediately give up trying to find a big issue to give my life meaning. I went on to sequentially dedicate my life to significant environmental issues, emergency response, homeland security, and medical training to save lives. Those issues ultimately proved inadequate for various reasons. However, the issue that has persisted for 8 years is to pursue the science of TSTG and to improve TSTG understanding. Thus this book.

The *isolation crisis* is typically resolved by seeking friendship and love to reduce the loneliness of isolation. Until a TSTG decides to come out at least partially, the isolation crisis cannot be resolved. This is because the TSTG must remain on guard to protect their secret which, as we have seen, creates loneliness and stifles authenticity. I addressed this loneliness in Chapters 1 and 2 for which time periods the loneliness was most intense but for me some loneliness still persists. There people in my personal life to whom I have not come out.

The resolution of the *free will crisis* involves the perceived realization that one is responsible for the state of the world because you can choose to do something about it. You have a responsibility to change the world if you do not like it. Although people perceive themselves as having free will and respond to this crisis, in fact free will is an illusion that we will explore next.

The issue of free will versus choice is often used to batter TSTG by saying that TSTG is obviously "just" a lifestyle choice. The argument is based on the idea that humans have free will but, in fact, I maintain that they do not. Yes, you read that correctly! Humans, whether TSTG or not, do not have free will and we will review some of the evidence for this below. Free will and choice are illusions of our consciousness. Although, as I pointed out above, people frequently have free will crises that they have to resolve and may motivate them to beneficially change behavior, the actual resolution of this crisis is predetermined by unconscious mechanisms in our nervous system that have already made the choice.

Our nervous system consists of mechanisms that are nearly completely unconscious. They are literally "out of control" (Kelly, 1995). For example, the hypothalamus and brain stem have mechanisms that control temperature regulation and hormonal regulation. Other mechanisms coordinate walking and riding a bicycle or motion sickness. As we saw in Chapter 3, the amygdala controls the hypothalamus mechanisms in order to prepare the organism for future behavior. These are the mechanisms that survived our evolution over the past several hundred million years. Some survived because they were beneficial to the species, while others just survived because they did not get in the way of reproduction. These mechanisms are totally unconscious. We cannot directly perceive them nor control them through what we consider conscious thought. We only perceive their effects through sensors in the body (e.g. feeling of skin warmness during fevers) but not in the nervous system. Another example involves the experience when we have motion sickness. The mechanisms that cause nausea and dizziness are in the brainstem and we have no direct conscious control over them, even though we would very much like to control them.

We often believe that consciousness and choice are real but choice is an illusion that is part of the illusion of consciousness. Conscious choice is not required for decision or judgment (Jaynes, 2000). Some of the early psychologists in the 20th century in the Wurzburg School conducted the following experiment that you can conduct yourself. Take two objects, such as a pen and pencil, put one in each hand and judge which one is heavier. Your consciousness can be aware of the pressure on your hand or the shape of the objects. However, your choice of which is heavier is already made for you without conscious awareness. Choice by unconscious mechanisms occurs before we are aware of it. As shown by brain fMRI and single cell neuron recording, choice clearly is established at least 1.5-10 seconds before it enters awareness (Soon, et al., 2008; Fried, et al., 2011).

Not only is consciousness not involved in choice, it is not involved in memory or the perception of a continuous visual world. Recall of words or riding a bicycle, once learned, just happens without conscious awareness. Consciousness of the visual world is perceived to be continuous but in fact we are "blind" much of the time. The eyeball is in nearly continuous motion and only takes "snapshots" when it stops. During the movements we are completely blind. In effect, our visual system does not make a continuous record of the world; it collects image snapshots that are strung together by unconscious processes. Our unconscious brain makes the visual scene seem continuous to us.

Why does our brain deal in illusions? Imagine our panic if we suddenly could directly perceive and control all of the mechanisms in the nervous system. It would be overwhelming and inefficient. We would have to have a much larger brain just to collect this information and control the mechanisms. If you were aware of all the mechanisms that contribute to choice you would be overwhelmed as well. Our processes of choice are "out of control." Our illusion of choice protects us from potential panic.

There is some science to suggest how choice might be mediated by unconscious mechanisms. Georgeopolous trained monkeys to get reinforcement if they successfully chose to move a joystick towards a small light which varied in position. By recording brain cell activity from the premotor cortex, he found that the neurons there seemed to be a "voting" mechanism for determining the proper direction of movement. The premotor cortex is that part of the cerebral cortex that cues the adjoining motor cortex to cause body actions. Neurons voted not only on direction but also by varying their frequency of response. Their frequency of response seemed to encode how sure their mechanism thought their choice was correct. This "vector voting" scheme seemed to predict the choice of the monkey in advance (Georgeopolis et al., 1988). Unconscious mechanisms all over the brain were involved in stimulating these cells. Since both the motor cortex as well as the mechanisms involved are unconscious, the decision was made unconsciously.

What about the human soul? It might influence TSTG human behavior if it exists. There are TSTG Native Americans who report experiencing souls with multiple genders. So a soul might be gendered. If a non-physical soul does exist, it would have to have a communication interface to the nervous system (Ryle, 1949) to influence behavior. An interface such as the one used in the movie "The Matrix" that plugs into the brain somehow would be necessary. It would have to be much sophisticated than, say, a USB connector and port. Here we encounter a logical contradiction or as Ryle calls it a "category error." Such an interface would either violate the concept of the soul as being non-physical or violate the laws of physical matter. Since science is full of discovery we cannot totally rule out that such an interface does not exists, but to date we have not found one. At this point we must assume that the perception of the human soul, though from verbal reports are experienced by humans is mediated by unconscious mechanisms in the nervous system rather than in some extracorporeal spirit. We cannot question reports of experiences with a soul or souls but we need not assume that they are non-physical. I should hasten to say that I think spirituality should be cherished; it appears to be one of the uniquely human functions that provide inspiration.

As a scientist, I believe in the principle of reductionism that means that, unless there is some intrinsic barrier, science can ultimately learn the truth about every aspect of the world. This includes how our nervous system works to produce behavior. Scientists have broken down many barriers that were thought to be impossible. Figuring out the human genome, once thought impossible, was made possible by large-scale computer organization of genetic fragments. Many in physics believed that we would never find the Higgs boson, a particle necessary to complete our model of matter. It was found last year by using the accelerator at CERN, the European Organization for Nuclear Research. I believe that someday we will have the technologies to understand how the human nervous system creates behavior. Recently, the National Institutes of Health announced that it would carry out a decade-long program to understand how the brain functions. We can only hope that some investigators in this program consider studying TSTG processes. However, they might not pursue TSTG research because they would be concerned about losing their funding due to criticism based on political correctness.

The scientific principal of determinism says that if science has enough knowledge, it can make successful predictions. In the case of TSTG, determinism says that we should be able to predict who is TSTG and who is not. Because the nervous system is so complicated, as a practical matter we do not have enough knowledge to predict behavior at this point in time or to change it. As a scientist I must believe that someday this will be possible. But be aware that we also need a public policy to deal with the ethics of attempting to erase or change the mechanisms involved with TSTG once we discover them.

We do not have perfect knowledge of the unconscious mechanisms underlying TSTG but, as we will find out some of the factors which are implicated in TSTG causation in the next two chapters. It currently looks pretty certain that genetic and epigenetic factors are causative for TSTG. TSTG results from unconscious mechanisms that form natural human predispositions for gender. It is not a lifestyle choice in the free will sense.

─────────── ❖ ───────────

The end of the Cold War was a significant life event for me that set me on a path to reengineering my life in many ways including being able to meet with other TSTG and ultimately to become a scientific detective to seek likely TSTG causes.

Chapter 6 References

Doctor, R. (1988). *Transvestites and transsexuals: toward a theory of cross-gender behavior.* New York: Plenum.

Fried, I., Mukamel, R., & Kreiman, G. (2011). Internally generated preactivation of single neurons in human medial frontal cortex predicts volition. Neuron. Feb 10; 69(3): 548-62.

Georgeopolous, A., Kettner, R., & Schwartz, A. (1988). Primate motor cortex and free arm movements to visual targets in three-dimensional space. II. Coding of the direction of movement by a neuronal population. Journal of Neuroscience. 8: 2928-2937.

Kelly, K. (1995). *Out of Control: The New Biology of Machines, Social Systems, & the Economic World.* Basic Books; Reprint edition.

Jaynes, J. (2000). *The Origin of Consciousness in the Breakdown of the Bicameral Mind.* Mariner Books.

Ryle, G. (1949). *The Concept of Mind.* Kessinger Publishing, LLC (June 13, 2008)

Yalom, I. (1980). Existential Psychotherapy Basic Books; 1st edition.

Soon, C., Brass, M., Heinze, H., & Haynes, J. (2008). Unconscious determinants of free decisions in the human brain. Nature Neuroscience. 11, 543 - 545

CHAPTER SEVEN

Genetics and True Love

DNA neither cares nor knows. DNA just is. And we dance to its music.
-Richard Dawkins

In any detective story there are usually several false leads that the sleuth eliminates after some hard, boring gumshoe work. So it is with the scientist. Sometimes in order to make progress, it is necessary to eliminate theories that "everyone knows to be true" by critically examining the evidence. New evidence pops up all the time and needs to be integrated into the broad analysis. In the first six chapters, we eliminated some theories that appear to be false given current evidence, but now we are ready to consider the considerable evidence that supports both genetics and epigenetic causes of TSTG.

TSTG appears to result either from genetic and/or epigenetic mechanisms. Genetic mechanisms result from DNA and DNA expression. Epigenetic factors include mechanisms that influence the brain, nervous system and body during development that modify DNA, alter DNA expression or are transmitted by parents separately from DNA. Although the exact mechanisms are not known, a dual causation theory is beginning to take shape. The "fingerprints" of a Two-Factor theory of TSTG are all over the genetic and epigenetic research and phenomenon of TSTG.

Both genetic and epigenetic factors do not have an "alibi" for the developmental time period when TSTG is formed. These factors start work at conception and their mechanisms could easily be in place at age 3-4 when TSTG emerges. Many of the other suggested causes of TSTG do not fit this timing pattern. To continue the detective analogy, they do not have an "alibi" for the time period when TSTG seems to be formed.

TSTG is not alone in having a suspected Two-Factor causation theory. The prevailing theory of handedness, the Corballis theory, postulates that non-right handedness is caused by genetic and/or epigenetic mechanisms. Similar Two-Factor theories are also under consideration for much more severe phenomena such as amyotrophic lateral sclerosis, autism, and Asperger syndrome. In the past few years we have just begun exploring how the genetics and epigenetics work and interact, and at present, we do not know the exact mechanisms for TSTG. But I believe that someday we will understand them.

The "smoking gun" in our detective analogy is the fact that the frequency of non-right handedness in TSTG is higher than the population. This telling piece of evidence lends credence to the possibility that some of the same mechanisms or similar mechanisms are at work for TSTG and handedness.

In this chapter we will discuss how I came to become a scientific "detective" and consider the evidence for genetic factors. In the following chapter, we will consider epigenetic factors and a Two-Factor theory of TSTG.

———————— ❖ ————————

A month after separating from my first wife, I found that I had fallen in love with a natal female who knew about my crossdressing and did not object. I saw her as a person who would save me from loneliness and liberate me from my secrecy. My professional life switched over from military and engineering back to biopsychology in a new city and at a university.

It was love at first electronic sight. I met my new love over a teleconference that was a relatively new development at the time and the technology was somewhat primitive. At the time, it was a technical feat that required two conditioned phone lines and a teleconferencing system costing $3,000 at each end.

She needed social science help from my organization and considering almost all of the members of my organization were engineers, I was the nearest fit.

We started a long-distance relationship. She lived in a city about 11 hours by car away from me. When I could afford an airplane, she would pick me up at the airport while I was crossdressed. We would stay home or go out and no one seemed to mind how I dressed in her city.

I had started taking testosterone by patch in hopes that it would help get rid of the crossdressing and enhance my sexual performance, now that I was getting on in age. I never thought it helped much but it did leave scars on my outer thighs if I left them on too long or forgot to peel off the aluminum foil that protected the testosterone. Even today, these scars sometimes erupt in irritation. I stopped using the patches in about a year when I discovered that Viagra worked just fine if I needed it and that the added testosterone did not stop my TSTG.

Our relationship was intense and it progressed to the point that we soon contemplated living together and marriage. Of course the logistics of getting married and living together were complicated by the fact that we lived in separate cities. We started looking for jobs in each other's city and started looking for housing. The idea was to start living together as soon as one of us found a suitable job. I won the race to find a job and it was a good one. It was very similar to the one I would be leaving. It would still be in military research and development organization and it was a promotion, but this one was associated with a university and I would have the rank of a full professor. The job was 10 minutes away from my girlfriend's house, a savings of at least 15 minutes commuting time each way from what I was used to.

The move to her house was uneventful except that she panicked when she saw all the "junk" that I had, which was consisted mostly of professional technical files, electronic junk and all my carpentry and metal working tools. I joked that she had married a fully equipped husband but she was not amused. That was the first time that I had seen her in an angry state but it would not be the last.

The move opened up new possibilities. The best of which was that I found a therapist who was actually expert in TSTG issues, one of a handful in the country. After a few sessions of diagnosis, her job became mainly one of patient management and discussion about what TSTG science I had found. She knew all the TSTG friendly doctors, lawyers and dentists in the area. She also knew how to deal with significant others and spouses. For privacy reasons, I again labeled my sessions with her as marriage counseling which was true and increasingly dominated our interactions as my wife's angry states became more common. The "walkabouts", which is what I called them, would usually start late at night when she would find some reason to reject me and try to kick me out of the house. I would leave and spend time in my car or my office or an all-night eatery and waited until she called me on my cell phone. That usually took 1-2 hours. I would return home and things would go on as if nothing had happened. I just figured that this was normal for marriages to have conflicts and I was particularly frustrating for some reason. My first wife had also gotten angry with me.

My wife actually allowed me to partially crossdress while in the house. Although when people came to the house, I had to quickly run upstairs to change. She taught me how to apply makeup and other feminine know-how.

The other new possibility that this opened up was that I had the opportunity to get a teaching fellowship at the university while the resident biopsychologist went on sabbatical. I had not taught the undergraduate course for well over 30 years, so I barely kept two chapters ahead of the students. When we got to the 2 lectures on the sexual behavior chapter, things started to get more interesting. The 2 lectures expanded to 4 by popular demand. The material did not come from the book, because it was not there. The 2-chapter lead-time over my students evaporated as I started doing library research on LGBTDQQA phenomena. In particular, the students and I were amazed by the unexpectedly high population frequencies for several of these phenomena. The latest biopsychology textbooks still do not have adequate information on these phenomena and that is one reason for writing this book

After completing the teaching fellowship and my biopsychology course, there were still some lingering questions in my mind. At the time I went to graduate school, there was almost no literature on TSTG causes but I gradually started to believe that things had changed some

35 years later. While I had been working to "save the world" during the Cold War, research had continued in the various sciences which constitute the domain of biopsychology. I did not know that there was relevant research until I taught the course but once I had a taste of it, I was on the case and would not stop investigating. At nights and on weekends I would research online and once every couple of weeks I would sneak off and go to the local medical library. This was no longer of passing interest; I needed to understand my life and my TSTG.

The investigation was not straightforward. But remembering what my lecturer psychologist friend from graduate school had said encouraged me to persist. He said that the physical sciences were like climbing a mountain. One can always see the summit where you are going, you already have your rock pick and ropes and the other tools you need for ascending the mountain. You have to fight gravity but gravity is universal; everyone knows about it. The behavioral sciences are like exploring a jungle. There is no clear goal, the tools are never available and have to be cobbled together, truth is often very localized and you have to sometimes cut through a thicket to get anywhere.

I periodically I would pull together what I knew, particularly when I had to give a talk. Milestones included a presentation to the International Foundation for Gender Education in 2007 and presentations to the Southern Comfort Conference in 2011 and 2012 and to the World Professional Association for Transgender Health (WPATH) in 2012. To clarify, the science contained in the early chapters of this book really did not come together in an orderly manner but each topic came into focus in fits and starts as I prepared for these presentations.

❖

In support groups I had heard rumors about inheritability. TSTG brothers and father-sons and cousins had discovered each other were TSTG, sometimes in peculiar locations like the local TSTG-friendly gay bars or support groups. While others learned about their TSTG relatives through family grapevines but did not make connections because they were afraid that their own secret might be revealed. Until I started digging, I had never seen any scientific papers on the DNA inheritability of TSTG and assumed that there was none. Then I found some tantalizing incidental reports of TSTG running in families in the clinical literature (Green, 2000) and continued the search.

Genetic causes are appealing because they fit some of the facts about TSTG that we earlier cited. The onset of TSTG usually occurs at the age of 3-4 that does not leave much time for causes other than genetics and epigenetics. Genetic causes also are compatible with the persistence of TSTG throughout a person's lifetime.

It should be stated that some of those coincidental discoveries that relatives were TSTG could have been by chance. Until recently, most people including TSTG thought that TSTG was very rare but as we cited in Chapter 1, both TS and TG are more common than previously thought. This was because most of the previous estimates depended on counting those TSTG who showed up at mental health clinics or providers. Estimates from these sources would be expected to be low. Most TSTG never go to a mental health professional and have no desire to do so, resulting in an undercount.

Traditionally the first thing that psychologists and other scientists look for as evidence of inheritability are the results of so-called "twin studies." Such studies have been done for many traits including intelligence, eye color and TSTG. Identical and fraternal twins find themselves in great demand for such studies.

The twin studies that I found indicated there was a good likelihood that if one twin is TSTG, then the other will be as well. The figure of merit in inheritability often used is the coefficient of concordance or the correlation between two twins which ranges from zero with no relation to 1.0 of complete correlation; the bigger the number the stronger the relationship. For this statistic, genetic factors are expected to have values near or above .4-.5 for familial inheritance. TSTG twin studies provide coefficients of concordance ranging from .50-.57 for MTF and .37-.40 for FTM (Bailey, 2000) in one study and .62 in another for both MTF and FTM (Coolidge, 2002). The correlation is not as strong as the correlation of intelligence test results that is about .75-.85, indicating that other factors may be at work. So, TSTG passes the "twin study" test for DNA inheritability but there is still room for epigenetic factors.

The next requirement one looks at for, as proof of inheritability is to see if there are genetic markers for a trait. A genetic marker is a chemical sequence in a particular location on the DNA molecule that, in this case, is present in TSTG but not in non-TSTG. TSTG passes this test with the discovery that some genetic markers have been found. MTF TSTG markers were found in the genetic code responsible for forming the androgen receptor (Hare, Bernard, Sánchez, Baird, Vilain, Kennedy, Harley, 2009) and estrogen receptor (Henningsson, 2005). DNA markers have also been found for FTM TSTG in a sex hormone metabolism gene (Bentz, 2008). Markers are found by comparing the DNA of TSTG with non-TSTG and due to the effort required at the time, one could not easily look everywhere in the DNA at the time. Like the man at night looking for his lost keys where the light is good, one has to guess where to look. (However, only a few years later it has become feasible to perform a total DNA survey; one for homosexuality has already been completed.) There are probably other markers in other places. Correlation does not always imply causation but at least finding genetic markers provide an existence proof. If none had been found, the inheritability of TSTG from DNA would be suspect. These marker studies need to be replicated and expanded because subject selection is difficult in such studies. It is too easy to select groups that differ in more than TSTG.

Contrary to what most people think, DNA can vary from place to place in the body and this opens up the possibility that the brain and nervous system could have a different DNA from the rest of the body with different gender predisposition. In most cases the body rejects a second DNA as foreign. However, the brain and nervous system seem to be sanctuaries in which multiple DNA can coexist. The brain, unlike other body structures typically consists of a mosaic of cells that differ in terms of DNA (Rehen et al., 2005; Galfalvy, 2003; Yurov et al., 2007).

The different kinds of DNA that form the brain and nervous system have been shown to be associated with differences in sexual development (Yurov et al., 2007). It is therefore quite possible for the brain to have DNA cells that differ in gender predisposition or other characteristics that are different from other brain cells and the body.

One way that we find out about multiple genes in the body is to study folks called "mosaics", especially those who are called tetragametic chimeras. Mosaickism simply means that more than one type of DNA is present in the body. Mosaicism is currently regarded as a rare phenomenon in humans although it has been extensively studied in animals. Because of the increasing widespread use of DNA testing, we are identifying more and more mosaics. Mosaickism is generally caused by mistakes in cell division but there is a specific type of mosaicism, called tetragametic mosaicism that is not caused by mistakes in cell division. Tetragametic chimerism occurs when two human eggs, which might have become human fraternal twins, fuse during the first few days after fertilization. A tetragametic chimera therefore grows up with the DNA from two different eggs in their body. When the fertilized eggs start out with both male and female DNA, it is possible for humans to possess both male and female tissue. In some cases of MTF TSTG, the brain and certain peripheral organs contain female DNA while most of the rest of the body including genitalia contains male DNA. Some chimera may be TSTG although the number of recorded cases is currently too low to establish whether multiple DNAs can result in TSTG, but this is a logical question to explore. (Cui et al., 2004). It will be interesting to find out, as we discover more mosaics going forward.

New possibilities exist as we learn more about the genome and how it is expressed through cellular mechanisms. Recently the role of genes believed to be "junk" DNA has been established as modulating DNA expression, turning on or off particular genes. This opens up the possibility that all kinds of gender predisposition genes may be in every individual but expressed in different ways depending on the settings of DNA switches.

The natural speculation emerges as to why genes for TSTG might continue to be propagated through the population. As manifested by the Native American "two-spirits" who have more than one gender, there is some advantage to having a TSTG for the clan, tribe or group. In Native American tribes, TSTG were highly valued and probably provided a survival advantage for the tribe. Having talents and wisdom that incorporate both medicine, weaving, art and war making, TSTG were/are in a position to understand a wide range of technologies and people. Another reason that TSTG genes might continue in the gene pool is that, until TSTG permanently change their genitals and bodies through TS transition, they are usually capable of reproduction. And, of course, TG can still reproduce because they have not transitioned. Then there are the FTM TS who suspend their testosterone treatment long enough to have a child. A final reason that TSTG genes may continue is that there are many "late-blooming" TSTG that have already successfully reproduced before they fully understand their TSTG situation.

In sum, the evidence for genetic factor involvement in TSTG is strong but the exact mechanisms and patterns are not completely defined. There is room for an epigenetic or other factor. This can be contrasted with the current results of research on the causes of homosexuality. Although it is clear that homosexuality is passed on from family ancestors, neither twin studies nor genetic markers studies clearly support DNA genetics as a cause of homosexuality (Rice, et al. 2012). Investigators of homosexuality causation are now turning to look more intensively for epigenetic mechanisms.

I have tried several times to look up the family trees of TSTG friends and myself in order to look for connections with other TSTG in my family. One search dead-ended because the father of my TSTG friend evidently did not want to be found. He had been involved in some notorious toxic chemical dumping under an assumed name and had fled to Canada presumably also under another assumed or real name. His mother was a member of an American Indian tribe and I had no idea how to trace her.

Another family-tree analysis dead-ended because the roots of my friend and her distant TSTG cousin both went back to Korea. There probably is genealogical data in Korea that ties the two together but I am not a good enough genealogist to find it, let alone read the documents.

With regard to my family tree, my mother was an amateur genealogist and left me a mountain of data on my family and others. The first thing I had to do was to trace my family tree online to determine what papers to throw away. I found no evidence of TSTG except for a peculiar fellow who was a member of the Pennsylvania Zoauves regiment in the Civil War. The Zoauves wore a uniform that was straight out of the Arabian knights with bright colors, harem pants and fezzes. After further research I found that there were no less than seven such light infantry units in the civil war and dressing this way was a worldwide fashion trend for military units at the time. Wearing the Zoauves uniform was not a convincing proof of TSTG.

I still have most of the mountain of family genealogical data to analyze but I believe that, if my mother had actually discovered TSTG in her family tree, she would not have documented it for fear of embarrassment. We need to do more TSTG family trees now that it is less embarrassing to admit TSTG.

❖

It was during one of my wife's "walkabouts' that she told her children that I was TSTG. While it was fun and sexy during early in our marriage, she had become concerned that someone in the city social circles would find out and ruin her reputation. I was forced into a "don't-ask-don't-tell" mode on TSTG. I no longer was allowed to dress at home and I returned to the "dress-on-travel" mode of existence that meant that I had to keep hiding my feminine things. Also, no more support groups. I used to be invited by her kids to play golf and hang out, but not after she told them.

Telling your wife or significant other about crossdressing before marriage seems to follow a pattern which other TSTG have experienced (Erhardt, 2006). Initially they seem to accept crossdressing, even think it is exciting but then they start to think about the downside issues. They wonder if you have a hidden life, particular when a TSTG describes previous secrecy. They wonder whether you will change sex (as do TG themselves). Then they wonder if their true sexual orientation is different from their experience because they are attracted to you. These concerns may result in them trying to control or eliminate TSTG behavior or at the least results in slow burning conflict over TSTG. Finally, there comes the ultimatum and the relationship falls apart. I do not know how frequently this process occurs but I have heard the tales from many TSTG people. There are serial monogamous TSTG who repeat this process with each new spouse or significant other. Knowing this pattern, many TSTG withhold the information about their TSTG behavior from a new spouse. This sets up a big fall from grace upon discovery and the mode of discovery or admittance heavily influences the possibility of relationship survival (Erhardt, 2006). Given the potential dangers of a marital relationship with a TSTG, the number of spouses and significant others that stay with TSTG are amazing and tests of true love.

The next suspect in the detective drama to be questioned will be epigenetics.

Chapter 7 References

Bailey, J., Dunne, M., & Martin, N. (2000). Genetic and Environmental Influences on Sexual Orientation and Its Correlates in an Australian Twin Sample. Journal of Personality and Social Psychology. 78(3), 524-536.

Bentz, E., Hefler, L., Kaufmann, U., Huber, J., Kolbus, A., & Tempfer, C. (2008). A polymorphism of the CYP17 gene related to sex steroid metabolism is associated with female-to-male but not male-to-female transsexualism. Fertility and Sterility, 90, 56–59.

Cui Y., Zhu P., Ye X., Wu Y., Wang Y., & Yin H., et al. (2004) The mechanism of tetragametic chimerism in a true hermaphroditism with 46, XX/46, XY46.

Zhonghua Nan Ke Xue. 10(2), 107-12.

Coolidge, F., Thede, L., & Young, S. (2002) The Heritability of Gender Identity Disorder in a Child and Adolescent Twin Sample Behavior Genetics, Behavioral Genetics 32(4), 251-257.

Corballis, M. (1997). The genetics and evolution of handedness. Psychological Review. 105, 714-777.

Ellis L., & Ebertz L. (1997). *Sexual orientation: toward biological understanding.* Westport: Praeger.

Erhardt, V. (2006). *Head over Heels: Wives Who Stay With Cross-Dressers and Transsexuals.* Routledge.

Galfalvy H., Erraji-Benchekroun L., Smyrniotopoulos P., Pavlidis P, Ellis S., & Mann J., et al. (2003). Sex genes for genomic analysis in human brain: internal controls for comparison of probe level data extraction. BMC Bioinformatics. 4, 37.

Green, R. (2000). Family co-occurrence of "gender dysphoria": Ten sibling or parent-child pairs. Archives of Sexual Behavior. 29, 5.

Green, R. & Young, R. (2001). Hand preference, sexual preference, and transsexualism. Archives of Sexual Behavior. 30, 6.

Hare L., Bernard P., Sánchez F., Baird P., Vilain E., Kennedy T., & Harley V. R. (2009). Androgen Receptor Repeat Length Polymorphism Associated with Male-to-Female Transsexualism. Biological Psychiatry. 65, 93–96.

Henningsson S., Westberg L., Nilsson S., Lundstrom B., Ekselius, L. & Bodlunde O., et al. (2005). Sex steroid-related genes and male-to-female Transsexualism. Psychoneuroendocrinology. 30, 657–664.

Rehen S., Yung Y., McCreight M., Kaushal D., Yang A., & Almeida B., et al. (2005). Constitutional Aneuploidy in the Normal Human Brain. The Journal of Neuroscience. 25(9), 2176 –2180.

Rice, R., Friberg, U., & Gavrilets, G. (2012). Homosexuality as a consequence of epigenetically canalized sexual development. The quarterly review of biology. Vol 87, No. 4.

Wisniewski A., Prendeville M., & Dobs A.S. (2005). Handedness, Functional Cerebral Hemispheric Lateralization, and Cognition in Male-to-Female Transsexuals Receiving Cross-Sex Hormone Treatment. Archives of Sexual Behavior. 34(2), 167–172.

Woodruff, T. et al. (2004). Environmental Chemicals in Pregnant Women in the United States: CDC-NHANES 2003-2004. Environmental Health Perspectives. 119, 878-885.

Yurov, Y., Iourov, I., Vorsanova, S., Liehr, T., Kolotii, A., Kutsev, S. et al. (2007). Aneuploidy and confined chromosomal mosaicism in the developing human brain. PLoS One. 2(6), 558.

The Transsexual Scientist

Epigenetics and Transition

"The right half of the brain controls the left half of the body. This means that only left handed people are in their right mind."
-Anonymous

The curriculum for my biopsychology course dedicated a lot of time to the effects of hormones on behavior and the textbook had an entire chapter on it. There were hormones that seem to have a role in sex and aggression and hormones that seem to have a role in pair bonding and perhaps human love. The other prominent claim was that prenatal testosterone organized sex behavior in animal brains and subsequently stimulated sexual behavior in adult animals, the so-called Organization-Activation theory.

The experimental evidence cited in the curriculum for Organization-Activation theory rested on the particular ability of one investigator, Gunter Dorner to castrate newborn rat pups that were supposed to be analogous in development to prenatal humans (Dorner, 1974). The rats were given either testosterone or estradiol during development and the results seem to support the organization-activation theory in that testosterone seemed to organize male sexual behavior and estrogen seemed to organize female sexual behavior. I had done enough surgery to marvel at the surgical skill it must have taken but the more I thought about it, I started to get doubts that anyone could actually perform such surgery and have enough animals survive to perform adequate testing.

The work of Dorner on sexual behavior was suspect but not very meaningful to me until I discovered that Dorner had extended his organization-activation theory to TSTG. He had speculated that too much or too little prenatal testosterone caused TSTG and that led me to pay more attention to prenatal phenomena and eventually to investigate other "epigenetic" theories of TSTG. Epigenetic factors include those mechanisms that influence the brain, nervous system and body during development that modify DNA, alter DNA expression or are transmitted by parents separately from DNA.

In a discussion with a colleague, I also distantly remembered from graduate school that epigenetics had suspected involvement in handedness along with dyslexia. That really peaked my interest because I already knew that the frequency of non-right handedness in TSTG is higher than in the population.

As I pursued potential epigenetic causes of TSTG, I discovered eight potential epigenetic TSTG causation theories:

- Theory that low prenatal testosterone causes MTF TSTG.
- Theory that high prenatal testosterone causes FTM TSTG.
- 2D: 4D finger ratio suggests prenatal testosterone influences TSTG
- Post-natal testosterone levels potential influence TSTG.
- Imprinting theory of TSTG.
- Drugs and chemicals acting as toxic agents on DNA or on DNA expression to cause TSTG.
- Maternal stress on DNA Mutation or DNA Expression
- De Novo Genetic Mutation

Low Prenatal Testosterone and MTF TSTG

It was conjectured by Dorner that MTF TSTG might be caused by low testosterone during certain critical prenatal periods. Dorner provided no evidence for this conjecture. Since his studies dealt primarily with rat sexual behavior and not human gender behavior, there was no evidence. Rats do not have cultures, develop gender cultural norms, display gender behaviors nor do they engage in TSTG behavior. Maybe some of our close anthropoid apes have some traces of these phenomena but there is no proof of that at present. However, in the past, we have claimed human uniqueness for such behaviors as cooperative hunting and use of tools, only to be surprised by learning that our ape cousins also do these things although not in as complex a fashion as humans.

Low prenatal testosterone has also been suggested as a cause of MTF TSTG in humans as an explanation of how birth order might increase the probability of TSTG (Green & Keverne, 2000). The notion was that a mother's immune system responds to a baby by lowering the amount of prenatal testosterone in subsequent births. The evidence was that a group of MTF TSTG attracted to males had later birth order than controls. However, results for a similar group of MTF TSTG attracted to females indicating that the effect was from sexual orientation rather from TSTG. This is consistent with several studies that indicate that sexual orientation is correlated with birth order in males.

Fortunately, nature has provided us with a way to test whether low testosterone causes TSTG. The Kallmann syndrome is a relatively rare syndrome that results in very low testosterone levels unless treated but, as of 2004, only 2 cases of Kallmanns have been reported as MTF TSTG in over 50 years (Meyenburg & Sigusch, 2001). Chronically low testosterone levels do not seem to produce MTF TSTG.

HIGH PRENATAL TESTOSTERONE AND **FTM TSTG**

Likewise, it was suggested by Dorner (1976) that high levels of prenatal testosterone resulted in increased frequency of FTM TSTG. It turns out that nature has also provided a test of this potential cause of TSTG. There are people conceived with a genetic DNA anomaly resulting in the phenomena of congenital adrenal hyperplasia (CAH). This anomaly results in the adrenal glands secreting large amounts of testosterone starting prenatally. Once discovered, CAH is easily treatable with steroid hormones that mimic the body's natural stress hormones and which reduce the secretion of testosterone through a feedback loop in the brain.

The question is, for CAH females, whose brains presumably are bathed in high concentrations of testosterone from an early prenatal age, are they more likely to become FTM TSTG? The answer is no. The numbers of FTM TSTG are not statistically higher in CAH females than in non-TSTG females, particularly given the population frequencies estimated by Conway (Conway 2001-2, Hines, 2006; Meyer-Bahlburg, 2004, Bevan, 2012). Although the CAH females do seem to prefer non-traditional female vocations and avocations such as carpentry and sports, (Dessens, Slijper, and Drop, 2005) they become TSTG no more frequently than the population.

As indicated above, the first two epigenetic theories above involve Dorner and Organization-Activation Theory. The theory originated with research by Gunter Dorner in the 1950's for sexual behavior and subsequently extrapolated by Dorner (Dorner, 1987, 2001) to TSTG behavior. The theory goes that certain behaviors are "organized" during critical prenatal periods through exposure of the fetus to testosterone or estrogen. These behaviors are then activated by testosterone or estrogen in adults.

As McCarthy points out, it is time to challenge the Organization-Activation Theory (McCarthy, 2008). Almost all of the research in this area depends on neonatal animal rat studies for evidence because they are believed to be similar in maturity to humans. Because of the surgical difficulty, Dorner's studies have never been replicated. (A university colleague actually assigned a project to a graduate student to find out whether Dorner's studies had ever been repeated and found no evidence that they had.)

Furthermore, as I have seen for myself, both male and female rat sex behavior can be elicited from either sex without surgical intervention in hormonally aroused rats. In case you did not know or never wanted to ask, rat sex is conducted by the male from the rear of a receptive female in what is called "mounting" as it is in most other mammalian species. (Humans and some apes are the only mammalian species that do it face-to-face. Even elephants do it from behind.) But during foreplay, aroused female rats will attempt to mount male rats and male rats will passively wait to be mounted by females as part of rat "foreplay." (I spent many hours watching rat sexual behavior being studied by the graduate student next door.) Of course, they cannot consummate opposite sex behavior in this foreplay mode because they do not have suitable anatomies. Possibly Dorner or his researchers were confused by these "foreplay" phenomena.

2D: 4D Finger Length Ratio

Indirect evidence for the influence of prenatal testosterone on TSTG that is often cited is the "2D: 4D finger ratio." 2D refers to the index finger length and 4D refers to the ring finger length. The idea is that the ratio is higher in females than in males because of prenatal testosterone levels; males should have higher levels during prenatal development than females. The results of two studies do indeed show that the 2D: 4D ratio for MTF TS is higher than male controls and lower for FTM TS than female controls. While these results are interesting, the linkage to prenatal testosterone is tenuous at best.

It should be pointed out that none of the 2D: 4D studies involved actual direct measurements of prenatal brain hormones so proof is lacking that hormones are directly involved in the ratio or in MTF or FTM TSTG. To this day, the technical feat of directly measuring fetal brain testosterone has not been accomplished. And in any case, circulating blood testosterones may be related to organization or activation of sex and aggression but as we found in male Kallmann's and female CAH, they do not cause TSTG.

2D: 4D finger ratio appears to be determined by genetic factors and correlates with many other phenomena such as: maternal corticosteroid levels, maternal stress, culture, athletic ability, breast cancer and prostate cancer. (Lilley T. et al. 2010; Van Dongen, S. et.al, 2009). Both twin studies and cross-cultural differences indicate a genetic origin. Candidate gene locations have been identified including one on the androgen receptor gene. Thus, it appears that the 2D: 4D ratio is not a reliable prenatal testosterone level biomarker because genetic factors can influence the ratio. However it is also intriguing that the 2D: 4D ratio is also influenced by epigenetic causes such as administration of anti-epileptic drugs because as we will find out below, TSTG has been reported in adults who were exposed prenatally to anti-epileptic drugs. The final bit of evidence is that the ratio correlates with handedness. Thus the 2D: 4D ratio research supports the Two-Factor theory of TSTG that involves both genetic and/or epigenetic mechanisms.

Perhaps the reason that high or low prenatal testosterone and estrogen do not cause TSTG is that the nervous system is not dependent on hormones for organization of gender; it is normally organized genetically. As we saw in the preceding chapter, there is good evidence that DNA genetics is a factor in TSTG. Genes that differentiate male and female brains have been identified (Dewing, 2004.) and genetic development of sexual structures in the brain begins two weeks before the hormone secreting organs are organized. (Reinius & Jazin 2009; Mayer, et al. 1998). Thus genetic mechanisms are in position to provide brain organization or at least contribute to it.

Post-natal effects of hormones for MTF TSTG

Potential post-natal effects of hormones for MTF TSTG, involve two poorly understood phenomena. The first is the male "pre-puberty" which involves a surge of testosterone around the age of 1 year old. This seems to influence fertility. The second is a surge of estrogen in males during puberty that seems to coincide with the cessation of bone growth. Although the estrogen surge seems to be too late to be involved in TSTG, both phenomena need further study.

Imprinting Theory of TSTG

A suggested epigenetic mechanism for TSTG is that of "imprinting" wherein chemical gene expression modifiers are passed on to offspring by familial forbears as separate chemicals from DNA. Imprinting is governed by different rules from normal familial DNA (Mendelian) inheritance. It is an all-or-none phenomenon that can carry down across generations. Imprinting is suggested as a potential cause of TSTG behavior (Green, R. and Keverne, E.B. 2000), since it is consistent with the research of Green that TSTG have more maternal aunts than uncles, presumably because imprinted modifiers of DNA or DNA expression led to the early demise of potential uncles. To this date the Green and Keverne study has not been replicated nor extended which is surprising because a replication would be so simple to attempt. All that is required is a survey of TSTG to ask them about the numbers of their aunts and uncles.

DRUGS OR TOXIC CHEMICALS

External chemicals (endocrine disruptors, drugs) and toxic events can change genes or impact genetic expression in the prenatal developing child. The effects may be direct or indirectly mediated through the physiological stress response (Braun & Bogerts, 2001; Massa et al., 1996).

Studies indicate that administration of anti-seizure drugs to a mother during prenatal child development is associated with TS (Dessens et al., 1999). Such studies have small numbers of subjects and a larger sample is needed in future studies. Anti-seizure drugs have established effects on DNA expression (Waxman and Azaroff, 1992; Rosenberg, 2007) including the two anticonvulsant drugs involved in the Dessens 1999 study.

It has been suggested that the drug Diethylstilbestrol (DES) is a potential cause of MTF TSTG (Kerlin, 2005). DES was prescribed in the US to prevent miscarriages and for estrogen replacement therapy during the years 1941-1971. It is a potent chemical that penetrates the nervous system and whose structure resembles that of a hormone although it does not behave in exactly the same ways as a hormone. It was prescribed for pregnant women until it was discovered that it had adverse teratogenic (toxic) effects. It also has mutagenic effects that changed the DNA in developing children of DES mothers and ultimately on grandchildren and beyond.

There are reasons to believe that DES does not act in normal physiological ways compared with internal hormones that the body produces. It does not bind to the main estrogen receptor on cell membranes and is an established mutagen. Its mutagenicity is dramatized by the fact that it increases the susceptibility to certain kinds of cancer into at least the third generation. It is considered a toxic chemical and some of its effects, like mutagenicity, are clearly not within the normal physiological actions of hormones.

When the adverse effects of DES were first observed, epidemiological studies were undertaken to identify its adverse effects and to create registries so that those exposed could be later tracked for future problems. Epidemiological studies did not detect any involvement of TSTG (Kester, 1980) and the CDC does not list TSTG as an effect of DES. Unfortunately, those responsible for the initial studies did not consider TSTG as a possible effect so it was not established as a relevant question for the registry.

In suggesting a role for DES in TSTG, Kerlin relied on a study which involved self reports of TSTG of the 1-3 million suspected DES sons through a private website (Kerlin, 2005). Very few DES sons complained about TSTG on this site although the response rate may have been low because privacy was not guaranteed. Of the responses received, the frequency of TSTG was well below the population frequencies estimated by Conway.

No doubt this attempt at a private registry was well meaning but it lacked the formal scientific rigor that would be required to convince epidemiologists of DES involvement in TSTG. As a result, both academic and clinical TSTG researchers have largely ignored the efforts of Kerlin on TSTG. To this day, although the CDC has asked people in the registry about their sexual behavior and related issues, they have never asked whether the people in the registry are TSTG. I recently pointed out to a concerned NIH DES scientist that her results dealing with sexual behavior might be skewed because they did not account for TSTG and she indicated that they might look into it (Titus-Ernstoff, 2012). Her study group was evidently totally ignorant of the efforts of Kerlin and the common claims of TSTG that their mothers took DES. TSTG health investigations in the US have only recently become politically correct due to the efforts of the current US administration and the NIH leadership, so we might actually see a study soon on the effects of DES on TSTG.

In order to see if I was a DES baby, I tried to get the medical records of my mother after her death. As executor, I had the legal power of attorney to obtain them. What I found was that there had not been a serious attempt to preserve such records in my hometown. My uncle was our GP doctor and when he retired and left town, he gave the records of his patients to another doctor who had taken over some of his patients. When this second doctor retired, his records appear to have vanished. I checked with the local medical society and hospital, but neither had assumed the burden of preserving patient records.

MATERNAL STRESS ON DNA MUTATION OR DNA EXPRESSION

Maternal stress could be a toxic factor in TSTG. The stress can come from high doses of normal physiologically acting substances, toxic chemicals or extreme situations. Stress has been shown to cause changes in brain development (Braun, 2006), DNA mutation (Radman, 1999) and changes to gene expression (Massa, 1996). The presence of chemicals found in our environment which might cause genetic mutation or mutation stress is well documented. As detailed in the Environmental Chemicals in Pregnant Women in the United States: CDC-NHANES 2003-2004 (Woodruff et al., 2004) the load of potential mutagenic chemicals in pregnant women is high and includes pesticides, fire retardants, PCB, BPA and chemicals banned by the EPA in 1979 but still in the environment. These agents may be the source of seemingly "de novo, spontaneous mutations" described in the next section.

DE NOVO GENETIC MUTATION

The current accepted theory of handedness postulates that non-right handedness is a function of both genetic factors and *de novo* spontaneous genetic mutation (Corballis, 1997). This theory is of importance because non-right handedness and TSTG may have analogous mechanisms. *De novo* in this context means that such a genetic mutation has never been previously experienced in that family; it did not come from forbearers. A combination of genetics and genetic mutation is the best explanation we currently have for handedness

The Corballis (1997) model of handedness combines both familial DNA genetic and/or genetic mutation to produce non-right handedness. Handedness refers to the frequency of motor skills for the right and left hand. Right-handedness means that more motor skills are performed by the right hand. Left-handedness means that more motor skills are performed by the left hand. Non-right handedness means that the motor skills are divided between the two hands.

The Corballis Handedness model postulates that there are familial DNA gene(s) that causes reduced preference for using the right hand but that the same effect can be obtained through genetic mutation of a random *de novo* prenatal mechanism. From inheritability studies, the genes controlling handedness are believed to be on the sex chromosomes, X and Y (Corballis, 1998). Corballis believes that the mutations are *de novo*, that is, they have no relationship to DNA contributed by the parents. Genetic mutation could account for some cases of TSTG that occur without familial inheritance, just as they seem to in handedness and other behavioral phenomena.

The reason the Corballis of handedness model is intriguing is because it is a well-documented phenomenon that MTF TSTG tend to have less preference for the right hand or are left-handed. (Wisniewski, Prendeville, Dobs, 2005; Green, R. Young, R., 2001). In my case, while I write with my right hand, I draw with my left, golf left-handed, bat left-handed in baseball and divide most other skills between my two hands.

To summarize the evidence for an epigenetic factor in TSTG here again are the theories with commentary:

- Theory that low prenatal testosterone causes MTF TSTG:
  No evidence to support.

- Theory that high prenatal testosterone causes FTM TSTG:
  No evidence to support.

- 2D: 4D finger ratio suggests prenatal testosterone influences TSTG:
  Supports Two-Factor Theory of TSTG because both genetic and epigenetic factors influence the ratio

- Post-natal testosterone levels potential influence TSTG:
  Not investigated.

- Imprinting theory of TSTG:
  Original study needs replication and enlargement.

- Drugs and chemicals acting as toxic agents on DNA or on DNA expression to cause TSTG:
  Good evidence that they cause TSTG but exact mechanisms are undefined.

- Maternal stress on DNA Mutation or DNA Expression:
  No study per se on TSTG but evidence supports both mechanisms.

- De Novo Genetic Mutation:
  Possible but mutation might be triggered by toxic agents or stress.

I defined the Two-Factor Theory of TSTG causation in order to pull together genetic and epigenetic evidence on TSTG. DNA genetics working on its own without considering epigenetics, can account for a good proportion of TSTG occurrence as we saw in the previous chapter in twin studies of inheritability. Some of us may have a different DNA in our brains and nervous system from those in other parts of our bodies. The brain evidently tolerates multiple types of DNA that may vary in formation of gender predisposition whether linked to sex or not. We will know better as genetic testing becomes more widespread as a biometric. New genetic mechanisms are being discovered everyday. For example, "junk DNA" is now known to turn on or off DNA genes rather than being a random string and our knowledge of DNA expression through RNA mechanisms is just beginning.

The second factor in the Two-Factor theory of TSTG causation involves epigenetic mechanisms. Epigenetic mechanisms probably contribute to the number of TSTG cases that are not due to DNA inheritance. Epigenetics may work through DNA modification, imprinting or effects on DNA expression. For those who are susceptible, epigenetic mechanisms may tip the balance in favor of TSTG. It is quite possible that a range of gender predispositions is contained in all DNA. We all may be susceptible to a mismatch between gender predisposition and assigned gender category.

Thus the Two-Factor Theory of TSTG causation indicates that either DNA genetics and/or epigenetics may provide critical mechanisms that create our gender predispositions. These gender behavior predispositions may not be in alignment with our cultural expectations and rules according to our assigned natal sex.

———————— ❖ ————————

I had not planned to start transition when I did, only to crossdress enough to keep happy. However, there came a time when I was very depressed and my shrink suggested that I take a low dose of estrogen to help alleviate the blues. I was abused at work and had loneliness and depression. My company put me on a no-travel ban, so my opportunities to crossdress were limited. My shrink was convinced that a low dose of estrogen would help due to discussions she had with a famous endocrinologist. He was attached to a local eminent teaching and research hospital. He claimed that low doses of estrogen had been beneficial in many of his MTF TSTG cases for reducing depression and anxiety symptoms.

The famous endocrinologist was booked 8 months in advance for new patients. He also put his patient data into the same database as my wife, her first husband and most of the city. While I believe in the privacy of the Hippocratic oath, putting the information in this database was tempting fate. The famous endocrinologist was too busy to treat me anyway, so my shrink and I decided to try a private practice endocrinologist who had treated TSTG in the past. My psychologist wrote me a letter and off I went.

There was one peculiarity of this private endocrinologist, she would not accept health insurance for TSTG treatment; I had to pay the full amount for doctor visits and blood tests. It was rumored that some insurance company had threatened her about charging them for previous TSTG appointments and treatments that were not covered by their insurance. The doctor gave me the tests, read the letter from my shrink and gave me some prescriptions. I had the prescriptions filled outside of my health insurance to keep her out of trouble and so that the insurance company would not know about them. It turns out that my insurance company actually did find out about these drugs because I had signed a waiver granting them access to my medical records. My social security number was associated with the prescriptions in the drugstore database.

The results of taking her prescriptions were wonderful. I felt like I was floating on air and my nipples were tender, erect and delicious to rub. It was not until I went back to my shrink and compared recommended TS doses with my prescriptions that we discovered that the endocrinologist had not prescribed a low dose estrogen regime but instead had started me on a full load of TS hormone therapy (HT) medicines. There was estrogen but also spironolactone (a testosterone blocker) and progesterone in the mix. She had taken it on herself to put me in full HT. I was transitioning!

So, of course, I panicked. I liked the HT drugs and their effects but I was not certain about whether I was ready for them and their potential side effects that include increased risk for blood clots. As a result of my panic, I stopped taking the meds and missed my next endocrinology appointment. When she found out that I had missed my appointment, the endocrinologist also freaked out, fearing that I had gone off a bridge or died because of her medications. She called me and told me that I was not to miss one of her appointments ever again!

It was about 6 weeks before my rescheduled appointment, so I had some time to think about whether to transition or not. I went through existential crisis number one (see Chapter 6) that is the realization that one will someday die. I decided that I had limited time left in my lifetime and that transition was what I wanted. I had put it off so long, and the decision lifted a burden from me.

My decision to transition was a little easier because by then I had confirmation that my TSTG was not something that I had created or chosen. At that time, I had good evidence that TSTG was common and caused by a combination of genetic and epigenetic mechanisms. And I really liked how I felt, that female hormones circulating through me made me feel better. I took a tongue lashing from the private endocrinologist and started the medications again. She decided that what I needed was a temporary reduction in the doses but gradually increased them.

With HT hormones, breast growth started to take place and that led to me starting a blog. Breast development in MTF TS using HT does not currently have a predictable outcome. The TS fable is that a MTF will reach her genetic mothers size or slightly smaller but there is little data on this point. (After three years on HT, I am barely an A but my mother was a D. Try trying to find a 48A bra!) About 50% of TS do not get enough growth and opt for breast implant surgery. Optimum growth requires both estrogen and progesterone because they influence and cause to grow different types of breast tissue. Although there are some doctors, primarily in the UK, that do not believe that progesterone should be used in HT at all. I started a blog to provide scientific information on this issue. I concluded that progesterone did contribute to breast growth because it influences certain tissues that estrogen will not grow. I concluded that the risks of taking progesterone for breast development need to be balanced against the risks of breast implants that are substantial. Most MTF TS wait to see what they are going to get from HT before considering breast implants but some go right to implants.

The acceptable breast size varies by culture, so TS will grow or get implants to achieve these cultural norms. Cup size seems to vary from culture to culture, depending perhaps on genetic and nutritional factors. There is even a world map of average cup size in which the US is depicted as mainly a B, tending to C. Surprisingly, UK is a solid D cup. Most of the Asia is an A. The science of breast development is hampered by the lack of objective measurements of breast size and volume. Cup size as a measurement of breast size is flawed because it is subjective and procedures for determining it are not uniform. Instrumentation for this purpose has started to be developed but it is not widespread.

At first I did not believe the fact that MTF get more emotional on HT but now I know this to be true. I now cry at both happy and sad movies, and particularly nostalgic Christmas movies like "Miracle on 34th Street" and "It's a Wonderful Life." I even cry watching war movies, which I never did. The intensity of this emotional reaction seems to vary with the current dosage of estrogen. I am not about to change my dosage to run an experiment. I have learned that in HT regularity and stability of dosages is important.

I have begun to reengineer my life. I own a certified transgender business, certified by the National Gay and Lesbian Chamber of Commerce and indicated as such on my website, blog, Twitter and Facebook. I tell everyone as needed that I am transitioning. I have not changed psychologists but have changed endocrinologists because the new one talks to me and because he takes medical insurance. Most of the time I am in work clothes but I keep a pantsuit and skirt suit handy for dressy occasions. I have a makeup person at the local mall and a hairdresser who both know about me.

I have started electrolysis for my face that makes me unable to conduct intellectual activities 24-36 hours after each session. My brain feels like it goes numb. The pain of being a human pincushion for an hour is something to which I do not look forward every week but it still continues. Maybe it is the endorphins that numb my brain.

When I am not working on military research and development projects that pay the bills, I continue to vacuum up all the TSTG research I can find. I particularly follow developments in genetics and epigenetics that might point to more specific mechanisms of TSTG.

My wife's walkabouts finally subsided and we have been living happily together. I have grown my hair long.

Chapter 8 References

Arnold, A., & Breedlove, S. (1985). Organizational and activational effects of sex steroids on brain and behavior: a reanalysis. Hormones and Behavior. 19, 469–498.

Bevan, T. (2011). The Biopsychology of TSTG. WPATH Proceedings.

Bogaert, A. (2003). Interaction of Fraternal Birth Order and Body Size in Male Sexual Orientation. Behavioral Neuroscience. Vol. 117(2), 381–384.

Braun, K., & Bogerts, B. (2001). Experience guided neuronal plasticity. Significance for pathogenesis and therapy of psychiatric diseases. Nervenarzt. 72(1), 3-10.

Conway, L. (2001-2002) How Frequently Does Transsexualism Occur?, 2013. http://ai.eecs.umich.edu/people/conway/TS/TSprevalence.html

Corballis, M. C., (1997). The genetics and evolution of handedness. Psychological Review. 105, 714-777.

Corballis, M., Lee, K., McManus, I., & Crow, T. (1998). Location of the handedness gene on the X and Y chromosomes. American Journal of Medical Genetics Part B: Neuropsychiatric Genetics. Volume 67. Issue 1, Pages 50-52.

Dessens, A., Cohen-Kettenis, P., Mellenbergh, G., Poll, N., & Koppe, J. et al. (1999). Prenatal exposure to anticonvulsants and psychosexual development. Archives of Sexual Behavior. 28(1), 31.

Dessens, A., Slijper, F., & Drop, S. (2005). Gender Dysphoria and Gender Change in Chromosomal Females with Congenital Adrenal Hyperplasia. Archives of Sexual Behavior. 34(4), 389–397.

Dewing, P., Shia, T., Horvath S., & Vilain, E. (2004). Sexually dimorphic gene expression in mouse brain precedes gonadal differentiation. Molecular Brain Research. 118, 82–90.

Dorner, D. (1976) *Hormones and Brain Differentiation,* Elsevier, Amsterdam-Oxford-New York.

Dorner G, Döcke F, & Götz F, et al. (1987). Sexual differentiation of gonadotrophin secretion, sexual orientation and gender role behavior. Journal of Steroid Biochemistry. 27, 1981-1987.

Dorner G., Götz F., Rohde W., Plagemann P., Lindner R., Hartmut P., et al. (2001) Genetic and Epigenetic Effects on Sexual Brain. Organization Mediated by Sex Hormones. Neuroendocrinology Letters. 22, 403–409.

Green, R., & Keverne, E. (2000). The Disparate Maternal Aunt-Uncle Ratio in Male Transsexuals: an Explanation Invoking Genomic Imprinting. Journal of Theoretical Biology. 202, 55-63.

Green, R. (2000). Family co-occurrence of "gender dysphoria": Ten sibling or parent-child pairs. Archives of Sexual Behavior. 29, 5.

Green, R., & Young, R. (2001) Hand preference, sexual preference, and transsexualism. Archives of Sexual Behavior. 30, 6.

Hall, C., Jones, J., Meyer-Bahlburg, H., Dolezal, C., Coleman, M., Foster, P., et al. (2004). Behavioral and physical masculinization are related to genotype in girls with an; 89(1): 419-24

Hines M. (2006). Prenatal testosterone and gender-related behaviour. European Journal of Endocrinology. 155 Suppl 1, S115-21.

Kerlin, S. (2005). Prenatal Exposure to Diethylstilbestrol (DES) in Males and Gender-Related Disorders: Results from a 5-Year Study, *International Behavioral Development Symposium*. Accessed in 2013. http://e.hormone.tulane.edu

Kester P., Green, R., Finch, S., & Williams K. (1980). Prenatal female hormone administration and psychosexual development in human males. Psychoneuroendocrinology. 5, 269-285.

Lilley T, Laaksonen T, Huitu O, & Helle S. (2010). Maternal corticosterone but not testosterone level is associated with the ratio of second-to-fourth digit length (2D: 4D) in field vole offspring (*Microtus agrestis*). Physiology and Behavior. 2010 Mar 30; 99(4): 433-7.

Massa S., Swanson R., & Sharp F. (1996) The stress gene response in brain. Cerebrovascular Brain Metabolism Review. 8(2), 95-158.

Mayer A., Lahr G., Swaab D., Pilgrim C., & Reisert I. (1998). The Y-chromosomal genes SRY and ZFY are transcribed in adult human brain. Eurogenetics. 1(4), 281 – 288.

McCarthy M., (2008) Estradiol and the Developing Brain. Physiology Review. 88, 91–134.

Meyenburg, B. & Sigusch, V. (2001). Kallmann syndrome and transsexualism. Archives of Sexual Behavior. Feb 30(1): 75-81.

Meyer-Bahlburg H., Dolezal C., Baker S., Carlson A., Obeid J., & New M. (2004). Prenatal androgenization affects gender-related behavior but not gender identity in 5-12-year-old girls with congenital adrenal hyperplasia. Archives of Sexual Behavior. Apr; 33(2): 97-104.

Meyer-Bahlburg H., Feldman J., Cohen P., & Ehrhardt A. (1988). Perinatal factors in the development of gender related play: sex hormones versus pregnancy complications. Psychiatry. 51(3), 260-71.

Poasa, K., Blanchard, R., & Zucker, K. (2004). Birth Order in Transgendered Males from Polynesia: A Quantitative Study of Samoan Fa'af ˉaffine. Journal of Sex & Marital Therapy 30,13–23.

Radman, M. (1999). Mutation: Enzymes of evolutionary change, Nature. 401, 866-869

Reinius B.K., & Jazin E., (2009). Prenatal sex differences in the human brain. Molecular Psychiatry. 14, 988–989.

Rice, R., Friberg, U., & Gavrilets, G. (2012). Homosexuality as a consequence of epigenetically canalized sexual development. The Quarterly Review of Biology. Vol 87, No. 4.

Rosenberg G., (2007). The mechanisms of action of valproate in neuropsychiatric disorders: can we see the forest for the trees? Cellular and Molecular Life Sciences. 64(16), 2090-2103.

Titus-Ernstoff, L. (2012). NIH DES investigator, Geisel School of Medicine, Dartmouth college, personal communication.

Van Dongen S., Ten Broek C., Galis F, Wijnaendts, L. (2009). No association between fluctuating asymmetry in highly stabilized traits and second to fourth digit ratio (2D: 4D) in human fetuses. Early Hum Dev. Jun; 85(6): 393-8.

Waxman D. & Azaroff L. (1992). Phenobarbital induction of cytochrome P-450 gene expression. Biochemistry Journal. 281, 577-592.

CHAPTER 9

Conclusions

Causality. There is no escape from it, we are forever slaves to it.
Our only hope, our only peace is to understand it, to understand
the 'why.'

- The Merovingian, Matrix Reloaded

In any detective story there are usually several false leads that the sleuth must eliminate. Sometimes it is necessary to eliminate theories that "everyone knows to be true" and ruffle some feathers. Evidence would seem to rule out many suggested causes of TSTG but science should go forward even in these areas because science is a process of continuous update. Those causes that seem false today may, with new evidence, become the preferred scientific explanation. In determining the causation associated with TSTG, the main problem is that we really need more scientific evidence, not less. In many areas of the world it is not "politically correct" for governments to sponsor research on TSTG, just as many cultures reject TSTG behavior. In the US, most of the research is bootlegged from the practice of clinical psychologists, although the US government is starting to address some of the social aspects of TSTG. The "big science" funding required for proper basic and applied research relating to TSTG is not sponsored either because it is not politically correct or everyone "already knows" the answers.

Scientists are people too and they sometimes are personally attached to their own particular research areas or studies. I have observed this when I give a paper or discuss TSTG causation on the professional society list servers. I keep reminding myself of what my favorite psychology professor said in college, that "science is a social institution." If you are a researcher, please do not take personally my criticism of any particular TSTG suggested factor or mechanism. There is nothing more tepid and useless than analysis that does not reach conclusions or make predictions. I have seen this in too many TSTG review articles and I believe I have read them all.

While my analysis may be shot at, investigators who disagree with me at least have some targets. You can quarrel with my analysis but do not stop doing the research in whatever area you choose. However, because adequate research support is not available for "big science", we need to be selective about the studies we actually perform and selection should be guided by analysis.

There are over 60 suggested causes of TSTG. In my opinion, only a few can be substantiated and some never can be validated because they do not qualify as proper scientific theories because there is no way to test them. Many of these false leads result from an underestimation of the population frequency of TSTG. The literature is full of investigators who, upon encountering a single TSTG in a research study publish a paper claiming that whatever they are studying is the cause of TSTG.

To review, here is a summary of some analytical conclusions:

- TSTG involves a mismatch between gender behavior predisposition and the cultural gender norms associated ones assigned sex at birth
- The realization of TSTG usually occurs at age 3-4 because it requires knowledge of cultural gender norms acquired by age 2-3; for some at this age there is only the sense that something is wrong and the realization that what is wrong involves TSTG occurs later in life.
- Your parents may have screwed you up in other ways but they did screw you up by making you a TSTG.
- Because gender behavior norms for clothing and presentation are culturally determined, sexual arousal for such stimuli must be learned and follow learning principles.
- TSTG is not a fetish; sexual arousal for wearing clothes or presentations of the opposite gender eventually extinguish because they follow Classical Pavlovian conditioning and learning laws.

- Because TSTG is rejected by most cultures, TSTG either must cope directly with the rejection or keep their TSTG secret from the time they realize it; secrecy is toxic and interferes with relationships and authenticity.
- Sex and gender should not be used interchangeably in science or anywhere else; gender should not be used as a polite term for sex. Sex refers to organs and gender refers to behavior and culturally defined gender behavior norms. Other definitions and usages risk scientific and social confusion.
- Novelty is a factor in provoking sexual but its effects can wane due to repeated exposure and extinction.
- TSTG are not rare; at least .1% for TS and 1% for TG of the male population and about half that for the female population.
- The mammalian brain and nervous system do not have "centers" for particular behaviors including TSTG. The brain acts as a whole to generate behavior.
- As far as we know, humans are the only species that exhibits TSTG behavior because TSTG requires culturally defined gender behavior norms; but we have claimed human uniqueness for hunting and cooperative behavior, only to be surprised by learning that our ape cousins do these things.
- Because TSTG is a naturally occurring phenomenon and has occurred in most all human cultures and times, it is not pathological; it is true that TSTG often need mental health support to deal with cultural and family rejection.
- TSTG does not appear to be the result of too much or too little prenatal testosterone or estrogen acting physiologically as hormones; there is currently no direct way to measure such hormones in the fetus. Those with congenital adrenal hyperplasia are bathed in androgens from an early prenatal age, yet their rates of FTM TSTG are no higher than the population. Those with Kallmann syndrome have very low testosterone, yet MTF TSTG is very rare in Kallmann.

- There is good support for a genetic factor in TSTG because of twin inheritability and genetic marker studies.
- The correlation between TSTG behavior in twins is about .62 indicating good genetic inheritability but not as strong as, say as that for the intelligence quotient indicating that there must be other factors.
- Additional genealogical studies are possible now that TSTG has received more acceptance and people are more willing to admit it.
- Genetic markers for both MTF and FTM TSTG have been found although the entire genome has not been investigated as it has for homosexuality.
- There are isolated reports of MTF TSTG tetragametic chimera humans who have female DNA in the brain and spinal cord. In other locations the body they primarily have male DNA; if true, this supports the idea that some TSTG may be due to multiple DNA in the body.
- The brain is tolerant of multiple DNA types and therefore could contain one that differs from the rest of the body.
- There is evidence for epigenetic involvement in TSTG whether through gene mutation, modification of gene expression or transmission of extra-DNA information as in imprinting.
- Potential epigenetic factors include prenatal toxin exposure and maternal stress that can cause DNA mutations and alter DNA expression.
- Current evidence seems to support a Two-Factor Theory of TSTG causation, consisting of combination of genetic and epigenetic causal factors and mechanisms.
- 2D: 4D finger ratios are higher in TSTG, also consistent with this Two-Factor theory, because such ratios are believed to have both genetic and epigenetic mechanisms.

The Two-Factor Theory of TSTG may be in a class of several phenomena that seem to have genetic and/or epigenetic causal factors including the phenomena of handedness. As previously indicated, TSTG tend to be non-right handed, consistent with this Two-Factor theory. The primary epigenetic mechanisms may be analogous between TSTG and handedness, but they may not be identical. Two-Factor theory of TSTG might be analogous to the Corballis Theory of Handedness except that epigenetic mutations may not be *de novo* spontaneous as in Corballis theory but may instead be due to prenatal exposure to toxins or maternal stress. As we learn more about both genetics and epigenetics, the exact causal mechanisms for TSTG should be identified.

This book has focused on my personal understanding of what we know about the causal factors involved in TSTG but there are reasons why the investigation should continue beyond my scientific interests.

For one, TSTG is a major public health problem, not because TSTG *per se* is unhealthy or abnormal but because children who are rejected as TSTG end up on the street and those that manage to keep their secret are vulnerable to depression and suicide. After being rejected by their parents, family, churches, governments, potential employers and other social institutions, many TSTG turn to sex work in order to survive. We must correct people and organizations that reject TSTG and believe that TSTG is a "lifestyle" choice. If not cared for, TSTG sex workers provide a reservoir of various venereal diseases and HIV/AIDS. If not cared for, young TSTG who are rejected or in secret contribute to the suicide rate of young people as their attempted suicide rate approaches 40%. The estimated suicide rate of TSTG may actually be higher because some TSTG take their secret to their grave. Suicide is the second leading cause of death in people under 25 and TSTG certainly contributes to this public health problem. The US government has started to address the public health problem in some social respects but more basic and applied research is needed on TSTG.

Second, TSTG exacts a burden on society because secrecy interferes with social relations and creates inauthenticity. Long-term secrecy is toxic and interferes with creativity and innovation. The toxic effects of secrecy hurt TSTG but also their family and friends who share the TSTG secret.

Third, TSTG is not rare; it affects at least 1% of the population and perhaps up to 3-4%. If you do the probability calculations, there are several US states and many cities with fewer numbers of people. This makes it too common to ignore and magnifies the public health and secrecy burdens.

Fourth, in order to deal with public policy regarding TSTG, there is a need for transmission of accurate information to the public. We currently have too many media sensationalists and hate-mongers that make their living by dishing out pseudoscience that they often just make up. We must have accurate scientific information to deal with such people and promote understanding of the phenomena of TSTG.

Fifth, and finally, there is a need for scientific information to support enlightened public policies with regard to regulation of medical practice and insurance for TSTG. There is evidence from the San Francisco city employee population that it costs no more for insurance that covers the costs of TSTG treatment and TS transition than it does to exclude such coverage. The insurance companies would like us to reject TSTG treatment because they think it puts more money in their pockets but they actually may end up paying more due to effects of untreated TSTG including attempted suicide. Realizing the actuarial reality, many companies and organizations are increasingly offering medical benefits suited to TSTG.

———————— ❖ ————————

Until now, I have deliberately avoided potential conflicts and social rejection because my gender predisposition was not in alignment with expectations based on my sex and gender cultural assignments at birth. I always swore to myself during each lie, each avoidance maneuver and each self-enforced period of solitude that it was only temporary and that someday I could be authentic. But I learned the patterns of deception and denial by rote and so they became well-practiced skills that could automatically be executed. I rigged the system to avoid rejection.

The price I paid for these denial and deception operations was loneliness and isolation and loss of connection to my fellow human beings and not really to know friendship. It was voluntary virtual solitary confinement.

Knowing what I know today, I should have chosen transsexuality earlier in my life and fought for being my authentic self, no matter what the cost. The delay has cost me time, friends and productivity. I had several good opportunities to choose correctly but I passed them up, choosing to fight another day. The day to fight has now come.

www.ingramcontent.com/pod-product-compliance
Lightning Source LLC
Chambersburg PA
CBHW030937090426
42737CB00007B/462